The Road to the
BOUNTIFUL
LIFE

The Road to the

BOUNTIFUL
LIFE

Achieving Success in Financial Services

Harry P. Hoopis, CLU ChFC

GAMA Foundation for Education and Research
Falls Church, Va.

To order a copy of this publication, please contact the GAMA Foundation for Education and Research:

GAMA Foundation for Education and Research
2901 Telestar Court, Suite 140
Falls Church, VA 22042
Phone: 800-345-2687 or 571-499-4308
gamafoundation.org

Book design by Suzanne Schriver Graphic Design, Baltimore, Maryland
Illustrations by John Lambert, Lambert Illustration, Chicagoland, Illinois

Dedication

In writing a book like *The Road to the Bountiful Life,* which looks back on so many of my life experiences, one becomes reflective. How do you measure the impact of all the people who have shaped and influenced you? While there have been many great people in my life, I would like to dedicate this book to my parents, Peter and Angela Hoopis, and to my wife, Bea.

My parents provided me with a model of value-based behavior and a strong work ethic. They inspired me to go into business for myself. They inspired me to be the best I can be. Loving parents are such a blessing and should never be taken for granted.

My wife, Bea, took over where they left off 45 years ago. She provided a solid home base, so that when I came in from the storm I was safe. Over the years, she has been a loving wife, a caring mother, an adoring Yia Yia (Greek for grandmother), and the chief operating officer of the family. She has supported me in all my wild ideas and schemes. She has been a sounding board, critic, consultant, and my best cheerleader.

I have been blessed to have such wonderful caring people in my life. I dedicate this book to them.

Table of Contents

Foreword

When you think of legends in the financial services industry, Harry Hoopis is bound to be in the top echelon of any list. So what makes someone a legend?

Among business professionals, legends and icons are those who embody sustained and exemplary levels of success. They are the folks we choose to emulate. Babe Ruth and Hank Aaron are defined by the extraordinary number of home runs they hit; Bill Gates' inspiration, passion, and determination made Microsoft a worldwide household name; and Warren Buffet's clear and unwavering investment philosophy has made him a billionaire and his investors very happy indeed. So what makes Harry Hoopis? Well, Harry Hoopis!

The Road to the Bountiful Life provides a clear view into the inspiration, passion, and determination that have made Harry a legend in our industry. More importantly, though, these pages provide the information, the pathway — *the road* — for you to achieve that same level of personal and professional success. Whether you are new to financial services or a veteran, whether you are in personal production or leading a firm, whether you're at the pinnacle of your career or at base camp beginning your climb, Harry gives you his frank and compelling formula to achieve even greater success.

He has the résumé that commands our attention. Some would even say he has the Midas touch. Harry built and led one of the industry's premier financial services firms in Chicago, was a GAMA International Master Agency Award qualifier every year since the award's inception, and built a variety of other successful businesses, including a sports management firm, a pension administration organization, and a cigar company.

Meanwhile, he always made time to be active in and give back to our industry. He is a past chair of the GAMA Foundation for Education and Research and a past president of GAMA International. He was inducted into GAMA International's Management Hall of Fame in 2003. And where lifelong learning is concerned, Harry definitely walks his talk. He is a member of two of the industry's oldest and most established study groups: LIMRA's Research Agencies Group (RAG) and the General Agents Symposium (GAS).

Clearly, he loves this business. If you ask Harry to name the single thing that has given him the most joy throughout his career, he'll tell you that it's turning an individual's potential into reality. That is without question one of his greatest gifts. Within these pages, Harry offers you the same education, coaching, and challenge that only his reps and managers could access before.

Harry was serving as chair of the GAMA Foundation's marketing and communications committee when he asked me to serve on the Foundation's board. So I've had a chance to get to know Harry as a colleague and a friend for quite a few years now, and I can tell you that he leads by example. Harry is a student first, honing his craft 24 hours a day. He has said many times that every manager out there does something better than he does, and it's Harry's job to discover it and put it to work in his own business.

He is also passionate about the GAMA Foundation and its mission. In addition to being a Diamond level ($100,000) contributor, he has donated the copyright and all proceeds from this book to the GAMA Foundation for Education and Research.

On May 31, 2012, Harry retired from active agency management, sold his other business interests, and put all of his passion, talents, and excitement into turning the Hoopis Performance Network (HPN) into what it has become today — a world-class resource for the financial services industry. The vision of HPN is "to be the preeminent training and development resource in the financial services industry." Its mission — "Utilizing field-tested practices, we deliver innovative, web-based training for those providing financial security worldwide" — complements its vision. HPN's core values are excellence, growth, and creativity.

Together with LIMRA, Harry and his team introduced Trustworthy Selling Classic for veteran reps, and in 2013 they released Trustworthy Selling Quick Start for the initial training of new financial professionals. In addition in 2013, HPN launched the Advanced Planning Channel, which focuses on estate, business, and retirement planning. Helping advisors grow has always been Harry's passion.

Now enjoy what makes Harry Hoopis Harry Hoopis. Dive deep into this book. Highlight it. Write notes in the margins. Share its insights with your teammates. You, your family, and your practice can enjoy a truly bountiful life when you follow the Hoopis formula for success. It will catapult your potential into reality.

Richard T. Cleary, CLTC LUTCF
President and CEO, The Partners Network
John Hancock Financial Network
Chair, GAMA Foundation for Education and Research, 2013-2015

Business and the Bountiful Life

Reflecting on a 45-year career in the financial services industry can be a lot of fun. As you can imagine, it's also pretty nostalgic because we tend to remember much more about the good than the bad. Selective memory, I guess. As I look back, I am struck by how incredible my experiences and what I have learned and taught others really are. The coaching, convincing, cajoling — and even begging — that were needed to help people find their way in our wonderful business happened regularly. Joy, laughter, despair, and failure are all part of an incredible journey.

My journey started while I was a student at the University of Rhode Island. I was an accounting major because I always planned to be an accountant. My father owned a small grocery store where my entire family spent every minute of our lives it seemed.

Dad had an accountant who was very successful. This accountant had doctors and small business owners, such as my father, among his clientele. He was the only person I actually knew who drove a Cadillac and was a member of a country club. He was living what I imagined to be "the Bountiful Life" — which to me meant having the time and money to do the things you want to do with people you love. It was what I wanted!

He came to our house on the third Wednesday evening of each month to review the business books. Yes, even accountants made house calls in those days. For several years, we talked about me joining him after graduation. He had one child, a daughter, who was not at all interested in taking over his business. I, on the other hand, was very interested. This motivated me to study accounting, which I have to say was not as exciting to me as I had hoped it would be. During the spring term of my junior year, 1968, my auditing class was studying life insurance as an asset on a balance sheet. An asset, I thought? I realized then I knew nothing about insurance and needed to know more.

About that time, I learned I would have to take an accounting class in summer school in order to finish my degree in four years. This meant giving up my high-paying job as a construction laborer, where I earned $4.25 an hour. But I had no choice, so I went to the placement office to look for part-time work. It was there that I saw a sign on the wall in big print that said, "Sell life insurance part time," and below it, "$75 per week guaranteed in 10-week program." A few years later, this would be called an internship program, but in 1968, this was a part-time job! Sounded great. $750, guaranteed. All I would need was another student loan and some money from working at my father's grocery store, and I could make it financially through my senior year.

I called my best friend, Alan Nero, who I lived and worked with during the summer. Alan owned a small house on a lake, and that was home base. He asked me to set up an interview for him, which I did immediately. Alan landed a part-time job to sell life insurance, quit his construction job, and we decided to form a partnership and share our summer experiences. We both got excited about the business right away, and in 10 weeks we shared over $5,000 in first-year commissions! We thought, is this legal? We stayed on our part-time contract throughout our senior year and enjoyed great success. Over the next few years, Alan and I opened a district agency in southern Rhode Island.

I then left for a stint in the home office. It was three years, two weeks, one day, and an hour until I became the general agent in Chicago. Alan went on to become a member of the company's top 20 on several occasions. We just celebrated 50 years of friendship this year!

I made MDRT and got involved in management at a very early age. I saw then that the insurance industry could be the funding vehicle for everything I wanted to do in life. I could clearly see that with hard work, I could achieve my dream of the Bountiful Life, which I define as "having the time and the money to do the things you want to do with family and friends."

I built an agency in Chicago that I am very proud of. It is filled with great people, successful people with great families. It was a labor of love, while still being very challenging and difficult. I mentioned to a consultant I was working with in 2008 that I wished I had kept a journal throughout those years, and he suggested I start one then. I decided instead of journaling that I would write my experiences in a weekly email to my people as inspiration. I would recount stories of past successes and share methods that worked over the years as a way to inspire them to pursue the Bountiful Life.

This book is a compilation of four years, exactly 208 issues, of those weekly emails I called Forum Focus. The readership increased over the years as one rep passed it on to another. Readership grew outside my company and even included the children of readers. In the end, there may have been as many as 5,000 readers.

The pursuit of the Bountiful Life is about five things: goal setting, mindset, potential, systems, and attitude. It is a walk through my life and what I have learned over the years. So many people have had an impact on me, and hopefully this book will have an impact on you.

When you have finished it, I hope you will agree this book should be required reading for anyone coming into or already in our business, and especially anyone interested in pursuing the Bountiful Life.

With our common goals in mind,
Harry P. Hoopis, CLU ChFC

The Hoopis Rules of Life

In an attempt to make this book most meaningful to you, I thought it would be important to share what have come to be known as my "10 Rules of Life." They are my rules, and I share them so you have a better understanding of me and how I think and operate. You are certainly welcome to make one or more of them your rules, but that is not really the point. The Rules of Life have developed gradually over a period of about 30 years. For many years there were only three, and later there were five, and a while after that there were seven, until finally I completed 10 of them. Most of the rules came from business situations, but a couple of them are purely personal. To this day, I list them exactly as I added them and not necessarily in order of importance, so let's get going.

"Life must be lived as play."

—Plato

1. **You can lie to anyone you choose to lie to, but if you lie to yourself, you lose.**

   This was the first rule, and it came about very early in my career when I realized that some of my reps were fudging numbers to look like they were doing the work they were supposed to do to please me. However, when the sales results did not match up with the activity, I stated rule No. 1 as a reminder that we needed an open and honest relationship if I was to help the rep achieve the Bountiful Life.

2. **We are all basically lazy.**

   Because I believe this, I also believe that to become successful, a person must set up his or her environment in a way that prevents laziness from taking over. This is where good habits, systems, structures, and routines become of the utmost importance. All the successful reps I know have mastered this.

3. **The mind migrates toward that which is most pleasing.**

   Until we commit to fixed levels of activity, such as phone calls made per day or appointments kept per week, we deprive ourselves of the satisfaction that comes with attaining a goal. Often reps say that they didn't reach their goals in appointments kept because they didn't have the right type of prospects. The key here is to see someone — anyone — so you can proudly say, "I reached my goal, I made it!" Then the mind takes over and says, as long as I am going to do this activity, what can we do to make it better quality? This occurs in every aspect of our business and personal lives.

4. **People will always disappoint you.**

Perhaps this is the rule that raises the most eyebrows. People will remark, "Harry, you are so positive, why such a negative statement?" The answer is this is how I am able to control my emotions. You see, the rest of the statement says, they disappoint you when their needs are greater than yours or the organization's. By being ready for life's disappointments, I can have better conversations with people who do disappoint me. I can ask what it is that is affecting their behavior and, as a result, often end up having helpful and meaningful conversations with them.

5. **Bad things happen to all people both good and bad, but I believe good things tend to happen more often to good people.**

This may be my personal favorite because it addresses the kind of life I try to lead. Be a good person, and good things will happen more often. Bad things and sad things happen to us all, and this is my way of keeping a positive state of mind.

6. **There is good in everyone, and it's your job to find it.**

My father taught me this. Everyone has value and is important. If you can find the good in people, you will develop a very special power: the ability to build relationships on a strong, caring foundation, based on a person's strengths.

7. **Never underestimate the impact and influence you have on other people.**

Whether this is in your personal or business life, it's always important to remember people are watching. Children are watching, coworkers are watching. Do you walk your talk?

8. **Never let your family or others close to you pay a price for your lack of self-discipline.**

Who pays the price when the rep goes to the office to read the sports page? Who pays the price when the rep doesn't study for his CLU exams? Who ends up paying when the rep sleeps in? It's the people we love and are closest to. It's the children who as a result may end up with more limited education options. It's the children who can't go to camp. It's the family who can't afford a vacation at spring break. It's a spouse who has to continually make difficult choices about spending money. There is no reason to allow this to happen.

9. **To live life to the fullest, you must continue to learn and grow by committing to lifelong learning.**

The mind needs stimulation and must always be learning. If there is one reason reps plateau like they often do, it is because they lose the sense of excitement that comes with learning and applying new ideas. It's the stretch into a new market that gets the adrenaline flowing and keeps us challenged.

10. **Life is too long not to have fun!**

When people talked about life being too short it was probably around the 1900s. The average male lived to be 47 years of age. In order to remain stimulated, we must find the time to do the things we love to do. The purpose of this book is to help you achieve the Bountiful Life, which I define as having the time and money to do the things you want to do with people you love.

The Doorknob on Your Own Business

My family owned and operated a small grocery store when I was growing up, and I worked in the store starting at the age of six. I now realize that it was a form of daycare, because my mother worked there, too. I tended to dislike the experience, and it has only been with the passage of time that I have come to really appreciate what the experience provided me in terms of life lessons.

When I was 16 years old, I awoke one Saturday morning in February to find that we had been inundated by a Nor'easter, an extreme snowstorm characterized by high winds and heavy snowfall or other precipitation. Our truck was plowed in, and the roads were nearly impassable. It was decided that I would stay behind and shovel the truck out, and my father would walk to work in the snowstorm. I can still see my mother pleading with him not to go. The store was eight miles away! How could he do it? He could be stubborn sometimes, and this was one of those times.

We watched as Dad disappeared into the blowing snow. We learned later that once he got out to the main road, a plow truck picked him up and advanced him more than five miles, with a hot cup of coffee to boot. Lucky Dad!

> "For as it is not one swallow or a fine day that makes a spring, so it is not one day or a short time that makes a man blessed and happy."
>
> —Aristotle

Later that morning, I was able to dig out and head for the store. It was a tough day at work, having to deliver orders in those blizzard conditions. It seemed like everyone who came into the store needed to have their cars dug out or pushed from their parking spots. When the day was finally over, we were beat. Our procedure at the end of the day entailed me pulling the truck around to the front of the store while my father locked the front doors. It was a double lock featuring the biggest Master padlock I had ever seen. When my father closed the padlock and jumped into the truck, he looked really bad. I feared for his health.

At that moment, I asked the most important question I ever asked my father, and his answer had more impact on me than any other I can remember. "Why do you do this?" He knew exactly what I meant. Getting up at five o'clock every morning, working 12- to 14-hour days, 90 hours per week, six and a half days a week, with no time off, and never having enough money to really feel comfortable.

Without hesitation, my father answered, "Son, I do this because it is important to me to turn the doorknob on my own business."

I owe a lot of thanks to Dad because that answer prompted me to look for a business I could call my own, doorknob and all. As a role model, he taught me that it's worth the hard work to be your own boss. I often say that easy jobs don't pay much. And even though his job was hard, it didn't pay that much either. But what it did pay was the satisfaction that comes with knowing that he was determining what he was worth, and he was in charge of his own destiny. In the financial security industry, we get to do this every day.

Snowstorm Day Lessons Learned

- **No. 1:** We have an obligation to show up. We have a duty to work the hours we said we would work and not to look for excuses to take a day off.

- **No. 2:** We have an obligation to our clients and customers. If one of our customers had headed out in the snow because they needed bread and milk for their family and we weren't there, we would have let them down.

More than 40 years ago, a mentor of mine said, "Harry, first you must get in the business, and then the business gets in you." Indeed it does. In this business, not only do you get to turn your own doorknob — you also get to make a difference in people's lives in ways no one else can.

What Price Are You Willing to Pay to Be in Business for Yourself?

We are all products of our genetic makeup, our environment, and our experiences. In hindsight, I had a great combination of the three. I had loving, hard-working parents who lived to move us to the next level in the economic stratosphere. I was raised in a grocery store, where I learned many of life's lessons that came from the experiences of being a part of a family slugging it out to make a living. That's quite a combination, if I do say so myself.

One of the things I remember from my grocery store days was waiting for the customers to show up. If you've never worked in retail, then you might take it for granted that customers always show up. Well, they don't. This is what I look back on when I think about prospecting.

You see, in our business we never have to wait for the client to come to us; we get to go after the client. My father's store was located in a neighborhood in transition, and it was transitioning the wrong way. When he first opened his doors shortly after World War II, it was an upper-middle-class neighborhood. Over time, as the textile business left the state of Rhode Island, things began to go downhill. Over time, his clientele got older and poorer. Many were receiving food stamps and were on welfare, and a significant number were on Social Security. These poor but honorable folks were in a struggle to survive. They would come into the store in the morning, for example, and buy one slice of lunch meat to make their lunch. "Thin, please, young man," they would say.

As the month wore on, people would be waiting for the first of the next month to get their checks and restock their groceries. Because of this cycle, my father's business had a cycle, too. He also would have to wait for the first of the month for customers to come in and replenish his cash. I can still see my father pacing back and forth in the front of the store, occasionally looking up the alley as if the customers were hiding there, playing a dirty trick on him. And if one of the neighboring supermarkets ran a big special or gave out double stamps, he could really be in trouble. He suffered, but he still smiled. He was happy to be in business for himself, and that was the price he was willing to pay.

So here we are in Chicagoland, surrounded by 7 to 8 million people, many of whom are among the top 1 percent of all income earners in America, yet I often heard reps say that they didn't have anyone to call on. Do you have any idea how difficult it was for me to listen to that for the four decades I was running my agency? Do you think I ever really believed it?

The question is: What price are you willing to pay for the privilege of being in business for yourself?

Some reps choose to convert their prospecting business into a retail store, waiting for the clients to knock on their door instead of doing the knocking themselves.

Just look at a few of our many available resources — there is a great marketplace filled with people, not to mention sites like InfoUSA, Craigslist, Facebook, Twitter, Google, and LinkedIn. Many reps have great clients who are willing to provide referrals, yet somehow it seems we never have enough people to call.

My father couldn't choose his customers. I even remember him throwing a few out of his store. In fact, my father reluctantly had to extend credit to some so they could feed their families toward the end of the month. (Many of those people still sent my father small checks for up to seven years after he retired to pay off their obligations.) There was no such thing as bankruptcy for folks like these.

My father loved each check that came in because the extension of credit was a major source of conflict between him and Mom. My mother would say we needed the cash when she paid the bills, and my father would argue that his only advantage over the big supermarkets was that he extended credit. They were both right, but my father gloated when the money that my mother had virtually written off came in. He would say, "See? I told you, Angie."

So what are you going to do about choosing your customers? We added average income per fact-finder to our ClientBuilder boards, yet only about 15 percent of reps reported it monthly. Were they afraid of the truth?

Measurement improves performance. Anything we can measure, we can improve. Why not make a commitment to do this small measurement and face the music for your lack of great prospecting or your lack of courage, confidence, and effort? Make this the first courageous thing you change. Don't wait for the clients to come in, go to them. If you're not seeing 60-plus clients in a month, you are waiting for the difference between what you do and when 60 show up. Guess what? They aren't going to.

What are you testing, and what have you tried differently? What would you say you have done that is courageous? What did you do today to help your children get to the next economic stratosphere? And how will you sustain that effort? Remember, character is the ability to carry out a resolution long after the emotion that caused you to make it has left you.

Easy Jobs Don't Pay Much

If your job isn't demanding, it probably doesn't pay much. Our job is demanding yet rewarding. It offers both financial rewards and the intrinsic reward that comes with helping others. We are so lucky. But if you are making your job easy by not working hard, don't expect it to be high paying.

I would like to share with you the three requirements of a high-paying job. For a job to be considered high paying, it must have one of the following characteristics:

- **It must be done in a place where no one wants to be.** This includes the American workers who are in Iraq working on civilian projects. I have read about many who earn as much as $100,000 or more for jobs that would pay far less in the United States. But these workers are far away from home in a very dangerous place.

- **It must be a job that not many people want to do.** In many cities in America, garbage collectors make more money than schoolteachers. It's a necessary job, but not many people want to do it.

- **It must be a job that not a lot of people can do.** Neurosurgeons make the big bucks because there just aren't that many people who have the intellectual and physical ability to do their job.

Now how about our job? We don't meet requirement No. 1 in our business. We get to do our jobs right where we want to, in our home-towns. If we travel for business, it's our decision. We can be home with our families and as safe as safe can be. So our job does not fulfill the first requirement.

But it does fulfill the next two. You might say that not a lot of people want to do what we do. It involves sales. It's commission only. It deals with intangible products, and in the beginning, it's not a lot of fun. So I would say our job qualifies under No. 2.

And as for No. 3, it's true, not a lot of people can do it. It's been esti-mated that only 20 percent of the people on the planet can sell anything. That's one in five people. So if you are an insurance and financial services advisor, you are in an elite group. I would say that our job also meets this requirement of a high-paying job. If this job were easy, do you think we would have the commission rates we do? Celebrate your challenges. We clearly have the greatest opportunity in the free enterprise system.

So then why settle for less? Why show up every day and not try to get all you can out of this great business of ours? Why not help people while you help yourself? There are a lot of people out there who wish more than anything that they had control of their destiny, but the truth is, they simply don't. There are a lot of people out there who think they are worth more than they are paid but can't do anything about it. And there are a lot of people who, if they knew about your opportunity, would give anything for it.

The Privilege of Being Self-Employed

Somewhere around 95 percent of the people employed in the United States work for someone else, either in the private or public sector. I find this amazing. It's also significant that about 10 percent of people in the United States are unemployed. That leaves very few people who experience the privilege of being self-employed.

Yet in our business, we have that privilege. We are lucky not to have to worry about losing our jobs. Privilege is defined by Merriam-Webster as "a right or benefit that is given to some people and not to others; a special opportunity to do something that makes you proud."

Another definition is "an exemption from an evil or burden." In our case, that evil or burden we are exempted from is the constant worry of losing your job.

The advantage of being self-employed feels even more special in unsta-ble economic and workforce times like these. But it is a privilege, not a right. It is earned, not bestowed. It requires you to exhibit the sacrifice, discipline, and self-management skills that will allow you to retain this privilege. There is a price for success, and it is always paid in advance.

My father, like so many in his generation, served in the U.S. Army for nearly four years during World War II. When he enlisted in January 1942, right after the attack on Pearl Harbor, he was just shy of 32 years of age and had been married for only three months. He had lived through the Depression era, had seen his father die, had lost the family grocery business, and now was off to war. When he left for England, he told my mother not to break up the household and move back with her parents. He insisted that she keep their apartment.

During his 38 months of service in England, he was never able to speak to my mother, but they exchanged letters daily. He told her that he was coming back and that when he did, he would open his own supermarket. The difference between a grocery store and a supermarket, in his mind, was simple. A grocery store had one cash register, and a supermarket had two or more. He wanted at least two!

He sacrificed throughout the conflict, sending home every penny of extra money he could scrape up, knowing that when he returned, he wanted to get off to a fast start. When he returned home, he had enough money to fulfill his wish.

That store was a huge part of our lives, but at the time, I didn't realize how significant it was to my father, our family, and me personally. In my teenage years, it was a burden, not a birthright. To my father, it represented independence; it was *his* business. He knew that if it did well, he would do well. He was in charge of his destiny. I now realize how important this was to him and how important it was for him to pass his values along to me.

My dad wore a white shirt and tie every day. My mother sent his shirts to the cleaners because he wanted them starched and looking just right. Funny, isn't it, that in 40-plus years in this business, I never once went to the office during business hours without a white shirt and tie on?

One of the greatest advantages we have in this business is one another. You are in business for yourself but not by yourself. Leaders provide you with the tools, ongoing education, and services you need to be successful. Follow this thinking, and you will never have to wait for a raise, look for a job, or ask the boss for a vacation day. Being part of our industry is very much a privilege, and the sooner you treat it like one, the more successful you will be.

What Is Your Purpose?

Before I retired, my purpose was to lead a world-class organization that has worldwide impact on the industry, while spending more time with my family and friends. And so I ask you, what is your purpose?

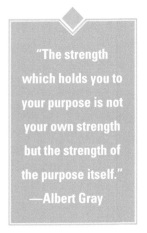

"The strength which holds you to your purpose is not your own strength but the strength of the purpose itself."

—Albert Gray

At the annual convention of the National Association of Life Underwriters in 1940, Albert Gray, an official of the Prudential Insurance Company of America, delivered a legendary presentation titled "The Common Denominator of Success." In it, he said, "The strength which holds you to your purpose is not your own strength but the strength of the purpose itself." What is your purpose? What drives you? What really gets you going in the morning? What is your mission?

There is a part of my family background that I would like to share here because it says so much about the price people are willing to pay for success. It is a story that defines America. It is a story that is probably true for millions of Americans, but one that is easily forgotten. In the hopes that this story might inspire someone to reconsider his or her own achievements, or lack thereof, I will tell it.

My purpose has always been to — in some small way — show the gratitude I feel for my grandparents, who made great sacrifices so that eventually I would have a better opportunity in life. When they made these sacrifices, they didn't even know me yet. Likewise, many of my sacrifices, while small in comparison to theirs, were made before I had grand-children, and now they, too, will be better off someday as a result. As you read this story, I ask again that you think about your own purpose.

I am from Greek and Italian ancestry. I know what you are thinking — how did I get so lucky? My Italian grandfather, Michael Taraborelli, is the reason that I am an American. In 1904, he decided his family would have a greater opportunity in America. He had just married and had one son. He saved enough money to buy a ticket to America, by boat of course, and with a third-grade education and little knowledge of the English language, he came to America alone.

Once he arrived, he found a job. For three years, he worked hard to save enough money to bring his young bride and son over to America. He went all that time without seeing his wife and child. Can you imagine the sacrifices they both made to improve their lives and the lives of their children, as well as the grandchildren they didn't even know yet? Can you imagine doing anything close to that? These courageous people, and many more like them, made America the place it is today. America became a melting pot of courageous people of all nationalities, people with goals and dreams, and the tenacity and perseverance to see them through. It wasn't just about buying a new car or taking a vacation. It was about lifestyle and independence.

I don't know how they did it, but their brave actions set the stage for my success. I look at my family today, happy to be in America, taking advantage of all the benefits my grandfather had in mind for us. What an opportunity. Then I ask, "What can I do to give future generations of the Hoopis family the same opportunity? What have I done that someone would call great? What has purpose?"

Shortly after I shared that story about my grandparents with some of my top producers in an email, I received the following response from one of them, and it really inspired me:

"Hi Harry,

As you were telling your story, it so reminded me of my situation, and the reason why I have worked so hard to make it in this business. I was born in Sicily, and when I was 15 years old, my mother sold her engagement ring so she could purchase two one-way tickets for myself and my 16-year-old sister to come to America (on a plane, not a boat!).

After we arrived, we went to different houses to live for the next 18 months. We had $5.00 to our name when we landed at Kennedy Airport, but we had a dream that we could have a better life here if we took advantage of the opportunities that my parents had envisioned. Through lots of struggles and long days and nights, we were all finally reunited as a family and have made the most out of the opportunities that have been presented.

I, too, think about what I can provide for my children and generations to come to make their lives better, and I thank God every day that I have found this industry to help me provide for my family and provide me guidance on how to do that. Thank you. Have a great day."

What have *you* done to ensure that your family will take the next step? What goals do you have to motivate you? Are you going to advance your family in the economic stratosphere? What are you willing to do?

I look back at what others did — the sacrifices they made — so that one day I might do more, and I cry for the opportunity to pay it forward. If you feel no one did it for you, it's time to take control and do it for someone else going forward. In comparison to our fearless forefathers, we are weak when we can't make that next phone call, ask for another referral, or go that extra mile. Here is what I often said to myself while smiling at my producers: "My grandfather took a chance that must have felt like getting in a rocket and going to the moon, and you can't even make a simple phone call to a prospect?"

Do you have the courage to make it happen?

Is it important for you to turn the doorknob on your own business? Are you willing to make the sacrifices necessary to make it work? Do you have a passion for what you do and a real sense of purpose? Is your work a mission for you?

> Your ability to embrace the spirit of entrepreneurship is the essential ingredient to your personal success.

Having the privilege of running your own business and getting what you want out of life means that you must do whatever it takes to make your business successful. This business we're in allows us to make a real and significant difference in the lives of others, while providing a funding vehicle for everything you want to get out of life.

Your ability to embrace this spirit of entrepreneurship is the essential ingredient to your personal success and pursuit of the Bountiful Life.

This Great Industry

2

We work in an industry that requires little up-front investment, offers unparalleled independence plus corporate benefits, rewards us financially according to how hard we work, and provides us with the satisfaction of knowing that we are helping our clients save and protect their financial assets. No other industry can match this tremendous combination of benefits.

"The first and best victory is to conquer self."

—Plato

Opportunity + Hard Work = Luck

Just call me lucky to have found this business. What about you?

There are certainly a lot of people in this country and world who aren't feeling very lucky in this post-recession economy. On June 29, 2009, Bernie Madoff was sentenced to 150 years in prison for absconding with about $65 billion of his investors' money. Imagine how those people must feel. Even with all the oversight we have, the crooks find a way. The other fallout from Madoff's greed: Charities suffered, yet Madoff seemed not to care.

And what about those individuals who wake up every morning, wondering if today is the day they will lose their job? Over the past few years, we've been hearing of more and more people who have lost careers they liked and believed in, with companies they liked and believed in. But, despite their talent and best efforts, the companies went bankrupt. Retirement fortunes were lost. Think of the despair so many people experienced. According to U.S. Census data released at the end of 2011, Americans' median income fell to $49,445 in 2010, the lowest number since 1997, and the country experienced the largest decline in income in a single year of any recession since at least 1967. Poverty rates also rose to record levels: 15.1 percent of Americans were living in poverty, the highest level since 1993.[1]

[1] Suzy Khimm, "The Great Recession in Five Charts," WashingtonPost.com, last updated September 13, 2011, accessed February 22, 2012, http://www.washingtonpost.com/blogs/ezra-klein/post/the-great-recession-in-five-charts/2011/09/13/gIQANuPoPK_blog.html.

What about you? Do you wake up each morning thinking how lucky you are to be in total control of your destiny, or do you wake up each morning thinking how tough life is?

There are two struggles in life: the struggle for success and the struggle of mediocrity. They each have their own characteristics. The struggle for success — personal and financial satisfaction — involves hard work. It requires focus, determination, and discipline. It is the path less traveled. It usually goes against the norm. While people may seem to be impressed with your accomplishments, they are probably thinking that you are just lucky!

The struggle for success has the advantage of fulfillment, validation, and rewards. It is the joy of doing a little more for yourself, your family, your community, and your religious organization. At the end of the day, you have the feeling of satisfaction. It's not without disappointments, but you have the satisfaction of knowing you did the things you could control that day.

Then there is the struggle of mediocrity. This is the road most often traveled, not intentionally in most cases, but nevertheless it is the result of a lack of focus, determination, and discipline. People become mediocre because they believe that they are in some way like everyone else, they are OK. Nothing could be further from the reality of success. Mediocrity is about letting your family down and failing to live up to your potential. Over time, this takes its toll on you personally as you watch the door of opportunity gradually close. You end up settling for far less than you had in mind at the start of your pursuit of the Bountiful Life. This is what you must overcome.

So call me lucky. Yes, while not everything in life is perfect, I feel that, because of my chosen career, I have been given the opportunity to define success. I have awakened some mornings thinking I should fire myself today for not doing what I said I would do, but I have never worried about *someone else* doing it to me. I have taken advantage of the control I have over my life, and that has made me very lucky.

Everyone in this great industry of ours has that same opportunity. No more, no less. So as you set goals for each new year, think about these things. Think about the resolutions you need to make *and keep* so that you can break into the struggle for success instead of suffering through the struggle of mediocrity. There is a lot of room on this road because few get there, but once you arrive, you are in for the ride of your life.

When we get to the end of each year, I would like everyone to be able to say, "Just call me lucky!"

The Five Characteristics of an Ideal Career

A few years ago, I attended a seminar in Dallas as part of my ongoing commitment to lifelong learning. The speaker, a Wharton School of Business professor, spoke about what people look for in their chosen career. He pointed out five characteristics of a career that are important to people, and I thought immediately about how well they tie in to our industry. Here are the five characteristics he shared along with my analysis:

- **Affiliation.** How compelling is your brand? How do you feel about it? I hope you feel good about your company's brand. What could be better than that? What could make you prouder? Be sure to articulate your pride in your company and its brand clearly and often.

- **Career progression and opportunity for growth.** This includes a career path for development. I hope you agree that nothing compares with the opportunities we have for growth. The best part is that you have the control necessary to make it happen. There are so many training opportunities and tools available to ensure your growth. Whether you choose to focus on a particular marketplace, become a specialist, or pursue a path in leadership, our industry has it all.

- **Work content.** The mission of helping people achieve peace of mind makes ours a job worth doing. Also included is the autonomy we enjoy in getting the work done and the variety that comes with each situation. Can you imagine any occupation that would afford better work content than ours?

- **Compensation.** We all know what an opportunity we have here. Approximately 25 percent of Americans have a family income of less than $25,000, another 25 percent make less than $50,000, and 31 percent have an income of $100,000. Only 4 percent of Americans make more than $200,000.[2] Amazing, isn't it? I believe money is simply a by-product of great achievement. If we do our job of providing peace of mind, we will have plenty of money. In fact, if you're in this business and you're not aiming for $200,000 in annual income, you've chosen the wrong career.

- **Benefits.** We enjoy the best of both worlds — the independence of owning our own business and the perks of being an employee. I want you to think about how lucky we are to have such a fulfilling career, one that meets all the criteria of a great job. It is fragile. Left alone, it

---

[2] *Income, Poverty, and Health Insurance Coverage in the United States: 2009, Current Population Reports.*

will shrivel and die. But with your energy and commitment, wonderful things are possible.

The Perfect Opportunity

I recently read *Outliers: The Story of Success* by Malcolm Gladwell and recommend it to anyone interested in success.[3]

One of the quotes from the book that really stood out to me is this old proverb: "No one who can rise before dawn three hundred and sixty days a year fails to make his family rich." What an interesting statement — it's kind of like the old adage, "The early bird catches the worm."

In the book, Gladwell says that work is meaningful if it has three elements: autonomy, complexity, and a connection between effort and reward. The bottom line is that successful people do meaningful work. What a great place for those of us in the financial security business to be in.

> Is it the work of our *profession* that is meaningful, or is it the work that you are *personally* doing that is meaningful? Because there is a difference.

I would say most of us would call our work meaningful. However, it begs this question: Is it the work of our *profession* that is meaningful, or is it the work that you are *personally* doing that is meaningful? Because there is a difference.

Being in a meaningful line of work does not necessarily result in your work being meaningful. For example, I can think of teachers who are indeed in meaningful work but who simply show up, correct papers, and collect a paycheck. There are people in every profession who behave this way. And while we might not like to face the reality of human nature, it is true that *some people work in meaningful careers but never do meaningful work.*

I believe that successful people are those who, given opportunities, have the strength and presence of mind to seize them. The ones who succeed at a meaningful level are not necessarily the brightest or the hardest working but are instead those who can put it all together. And, of course, we do know that working hard is what successful people do.

As I read *Outliers*, I couldn't help but think about my father in his grocery store and the sacrifices he made to provide a better living for us. But my father, while often very tired, was always happy in his work. I realized many years later that while his work was difficult and not that financially

[3] Malcolm Gladwell, *Outliers: The Story of Success* (New York: Little, Brown and Company, 2008).

rewarding, he had a sense of control, pride, and accomplishment because he was doing something that not everyone could do — organize and run his own business. He was the boss! I realized that my father was so happy in his work because it had all three of the elements Gladwell says must be present for work to be meaningful: autonomy, complexity, and a connection between effort and reward.

Let's look at each one of these elements more closely.

Autonomy

The word "autonomy" comes from the Greek words, "auto," which means "self," and "nomos," which means "law." It is defined as self-governance, independence or freedom, or the will of one's actions or living by one's own laws. Do you see how important autonomy is? It's about our ability to run our own lives and to set up the necessary rules, habits, and methods. We have that ability, and it is the first ingredient in a meaningful career. *A career in our industry measures up 100 percent in this area. The question is, do you?*

> Autonomy is not about flexibility, but rather it is about achievement and opportunity.

Autonomy doesn't mean you work alone, and it doesn't mean you are independent. Autonomy means you are responsible for getting the job done. It means not looking for anyone to blame. Autonomy means there is no room for excuses. Autonomy is about believing in a process and executing it on a consistent basis. Autonomy is not about flexibility, but rather it is about achievement and opportunity.

My father never had anyone to blame, but he did have people to manage. He knew he had to have employees to get it done. He knew that even in his little store with only two cash registers, one person alone could not make it happen. Autonomy allows you to share your dreams, systems, and methods with others who buy in.

As an agency leader, I always said it was my job to create an environment in which reps can grow and continue to develop personally, professionally, and financially.

We must take charge of our situation, establish daily activity rules, and follow them. In a session with LIMRA International, we set up a few panels and asked reps what they did to create the right habits. One top new advisor, who wrote 200-plus lives, gained 100-plus new clients, and wrote $300,000 of premium in his third year as his company's gold winner, said this: "My phoning time is sacred. Nothing keeps me from the phone between 9:00 and 10:00 a.m. Nothing! Second, I do not check messages during the day. That's it!"

How's that for autonomy? Simple and powerful. I see some reps checking emails almost minute to minute all day long.

My job is not to force you or your staff to do the job. It is to encourage you to do the things you must do to be successful. It is your job to take the things you have learned and make them work for you. In our world, interdependence creates the environment that allows us to exert maximum, focused autonomy.

You don't get too many chances at autonomy. If you want to be in charge of your own destiny, figure out the job to be done and do it. If you don't, someone else will, and you will end up working for him or her.

When I first came into this business as a college intern, it was readily apparent to me that this business provided the autonomy I desired. And although I majored in accounting and thought I would be an accountant someday, it soon became apparent to me that this business would provide an even greater amount of autonomy than an accounting career ever could.

So the first key to meaningful work is autonomy. To make it meaningful, it has to be done well and in a way that promotes high self-esteem. It has to be done at a level that is significant enough so that you know you've made a difference. And it needs to be done on a level where you can say you are truly living up to your potential. Your potential and your autonomy are somewhat synonymous.

> "If you haven't the strength to impose your own terms upon life, you must accept the terms it offers you."
>
> —T.S. Eliot

T.S. Eliot said, "If you haven't the strength to impose your own terms upon life, you must accept the terms it offers you." Your strength to focus on the right things brings you autonomy, and then you will reach your potential.

During my 44 years in this business, I recruited, trained, and developed many great people. It is those successes that made my work and life meaningful. But for every person who has moved on to success to enjoy the Bountiful Life, there are four times as many who have left the industry.

Why? Hadn't I selected them using the same questions, psychometric profiles, and other steps every time? See, what I couldn't test for was their desire to have it all, to never give up. The winners stand out after the game has begun. At the starting line, they all look great, and then life happens. The only ones who get to the finish line are those who are in control and have a personal sense of responsibility. They are the reps who value autonomy above all else.

When people leave our profession, in essence, they are throwing up their arms and saying, "I don't have the self-discipline to control my own life and future." They are then destined to give that control to another human being. Ten years after graduating from college, the average graduate has had about five different jobs in three different industries. The average 40-year-old male has had 11 different jobs.

The reps who take control will enjoy privileges known only to a few people in our society. They will never have to miss a child's soccer game or recital. They will have time to coach their kids' sports teams. They can decide when to take a vacation and how long it will be. That's autonomy!

Isn't it time to make a pledge to do the right things every day so you can preserve autonomy in your life forever?

Complexity

The second ingredient of meaningful work that Gladwell mentions is complexity. When I was growing up, I didn't realize the complexity involved in running a small supermarket, probably because my father seemed to do it so effortlessly. He knew what it took, and he made it look easy.

He always woke up at the same time and arrived at the store at the same time. Monday was the day he looked at inventory and placed his order for new goods. Tuesday they arrived, and he didn't go home until the shelves were stocked, and on and on and on. Isn't it funny that while I have always talked about *systems, structure, and routine,* I didn't realize for years who my real role model was?

I thought Dad just sold food to people. But it was much more complex than that. He was in sales, inventory control, public relations, and so much more. He had to know his competition and how to beat them.

Running a business requires diligence, attention to detail, and a commitment to making it work. And Dad was committed — so much so that he put our house up as collateral for his business loan.

Dad had worries. Every time a major supermarket with 10 or more cash registers opened nearby, it almost put him out of business. But he battled each time, welcoming his customers back with a bigger smile after each of their visits to try the big new store out. He never gave up, because failure was not an option.

This concept of complexity is something I also call "capacity," the ability to see all aspects of the job and to prospect, phone, fact-find, open, close, deliver, manage staff, manage money, and commit to lifelong learning. Ours is indeed a complex business — when done right. Your ability to keep all the plates spinning is the key to leveling out the peaks and valleys and enjoying a satisfying career.

The reps who are destined to struggle are those who, despite their talent, have the capacity to do only one part of the job at any given time. When they focus on prospecting, they get names. When they get on the phone, they set up appointments. When they complete fact-finders, they open cases. And when they close the sale, they get the check.

But they are caught in a frightful cycle of failure, never able to smooth out the peaks and valleys. Feast or famine becomes a way of life. Every day they come to work full of anxiety, for even when they are closing business, they know that as soon as the open cases are closed, they will be in trouble again because they have failed to open new cases.

I like to use a cabinetmaker as an example. This is a man who has crafted the finest cabinets ever made. Yet his business failed. Why? Because his business model is this: He orders the wood, makes the cabinets, sells the cabinets, delivers the cabinets, and then begins the same routine again.

One day, when he goes to the warehouse to bring in the new lumber, he realizes that he has forgotten to order new material. (This is much the same as a rep who says, "I forgot to ask for referrals." It's not smart.) The lumberyard tells him it will take six weeks to ship the new material. As a result of his poor planning, the cabinetmaker will have to lay off workers. The bills continue to come in, debts build up, and with no revenue coming in, the business must close. The great cabinetmaker must go to work for someone else and loses his autonomy because he can't handle the complexity of the work. Thus, he never gets to do meaningful work for himself.

> "Activity, even the right kind, doesn't guarantee success, but without it, success is almost impossible."
> —Al Granum

Now, if you are in our business, you know that we have plenty of autonomy, which requires that we follow the rules that govern what we do. The demise for most of those who are stuck in the valley of mediocrity is the inability to handle the complexity of what we do. There is only one way to smooth out the peaks and valleys in this business, and that's by maintaining high activity levels. But caution, activity isn't a magic bullet. As the great Al Granum put it, "Activity, even the right kind, doesn't guarantee success, but without it, success is almost impossible." High activity without a focus on all aspects of the business can still result in failure.

Can you do it? Can you begin to think of your business as more than simply selling a product to someone? No matter how good your process, unless you can see the entire scope of your work, you will never achieve success at the level you want or need to. So this is what is at the heart of the struggle so many reps face in our industry. You must put the systems in place and get to work. Accept the struggle of success. It's hard work, but if you make it, the view from the top is worth it. Trust me.

So let's modify my longtime saying, "Easy jobs don't pay much." Instead, let's make it, "Easy jobs don't pay much, complex jobs do!"

A Connection Between Effort and Reward

The third required element of meaningful work that Gladwell mentions is the connection between effort and reward.

What would you say about your relationship between the effort you make and the reward you receive? I think first of the money we make. That is significant. Then I think about the impact we have when we help people do something that is good for them and those they love, with the ultimate reward of knowing that when people die too soon, become disabled, or live too long, we are responsible for helping them save money and protect their families and financial assets. In this way, our career keeps rewarding us over time.

The relationship between effort and reward expressed as money is important because it allows us to provide for our loved ones. It allows us to make a contribution to our communities. It allows us to self-actualize. The more effort we make, the more money we make. Now don't misunderstand me, money is not everything, but here is what I believe: Money is one of many by-products of great achievement. And remember, there is no such thing as a poor philanthropist.

The relationship between effort and reward expressed as the job satisfaction we receive is essential to helping us keep going. Helping people save their money and protect their loved ones is an essential part of our daily lives. What could be better than that? I can honestly say that, in 40-plus years in this business, I have never met someone with a job that I would rather have, and now I understand that fact more than ever.

For my father, the reward was not just about making money. It was more about the sense of satisfaction that comes with making a difference. My father believed that his customers had a unique experience. He carefully selected the fruit and produce they would buy, and he delivered it to them with his beaming smile. People couldn't get that anywhere else. He didn't make a lot of money, but what he earned was his. He was proud, independent, and successful.

Gladwell writes, "Hard work is a prison sentence only if it does not have meaning. Once it does, it becomes the kind of thing that makes you

> "Hard work is a prison sentence only if it does not have meaning. Once it does, it becomes the kind of thing that makes you grab your wife around the waist and dance a jig."
>
> —Malcolm Gladwell

grab your wife around the waist and dance a jig."[4]

So there it is, the key to our business, right before our eyes. Yet some of you are just like I was when I was growing up: You don't realize how complex or meaningful your work is. We are lucky to do such meaningful work, and to do it with autonomy, complexity, and a direct relationship between effort and reward. Continually celebrate our opportunity by helping more people save and protect their money, and you will always do meaningful work.

A True Story About the Meaningful Work We Do

A few years ago, a remarkable story unfolded in our ClientBuilder meeting that demonstrates the meaningful work we do. I asked a young rep to tell his story as a reminder of the impact we have on people's lives every day. The third element of a meaningful career that Gladwell mentioned in *Outliers* is a relationship between effort and reward. When we sell someone one of our products, we are rewarded in three ways: with income, with the knowledge that we convinced someone to face a hugely important responsibility to his or her loved ones, and with the satisfaction that, when a client dies and we deliver a check to the spouse or other family member, the family will not suffer the loss of that person's income. Of course, that third reward usually presents itself a long time after the first two.

In this young rep's story, the final element came quickly. Here is the story in his words:

Back in March 2009, I was making some phone calls to general office clients and got in touch with a couple (43 years old) who lived in a town in Illinois that is about two hours away. The wife had some small whole life policies, and her initial questions were in regard to what options she had to access the cash values inside her policies (they owned a small business, and things were tight). I responded by asking them what type of coverage they had outside of these policies and did a needs analysis to find out that the wife had no other coverage, and the husband had a small universal

---

[4] Gladwell, *Outliers*, 149.

policy through another company. They were both making about $40,000 each, but they had two kids — 10 and seven years old — so I recommended that we apply for $500,000 for each of them. Like most people, they told me to call back in a week or two, as they wanted to discuss this decision with each other.

*I tried calling them several times over the next few months but could never reach them. In late July, the wife called me back to tell me that they were ready to make the applications for coverage. We submitted the applications on **August 14**. The wife was approved right away, as I remember, but the husband took longer. On **September 8** (the day after Labor Day), I received a phone call from the wife. She was sobbing, telling me that her husband had passed away in a tragic accident two days earlier. She immediately began asking me about the life insurance that was still in underwriting.*

After I got off the phone with the wife, I called the home office right away and began working with them to get the policy issued and hopefully paid. Over the next few weeks, I spoke with the widowed wife several times, the coroner's office, the detective working on the case, etc. The woman at the home office working on this case was awesome and did an outstanding job helping me through this claim.

*On **October 8**, I got word from the home office that they would pay this claim in full: $500,635 (the policy amount plus $635 in interest). When I spoke to the wife on the phone the next day, she took a deep breath (as what I was going to tell her in the next few seconds was going to impact her life and her kids' lives forever) and then broke down crying when I told her that our company was going to pay the claim. I got pretty choked up, too, when she repeatedly told me, "Thank you for being there for me and my family during this whole time."*

It was pretty powerful.

When I hung up the phone with her, I sat in my office for a few moments and just thought about how great it is to be in this business. Here, this client had paid less than $38 (one monthly premium), and the company was paying $500,635 to the surviving spouse — really, with no hesitancy.

For me, this has totally solidified the impact of what we do each day. It is our job to see lots of people and make recommendations that are going to protect them and their families. I feel very fortu-

nate that we were able to protect this family, especially considering that the insurance applications were made only a few weeks before this tragedy.

Thinking about my rep's story reminds me of an expression I have heard: "Physicians save lives; we save lifestyles."

This excerpt provides us all with an important lesson. For some, it's a valuable reminder. For newer reps, it's a powerful story to hold onto and share with clients.

Just think how different the lives of that family — a mother with two children ages seven and 10 who wanted to know how much cash value she had available because things were tight — will be because of that young rep's hard work and dedication to his client and addressing his client's needs.

The Equal Opportunity Employer

One day, a form came across my desk to sign up our office for a job fair. The form had a box to check to indicate that my organization was an equal opportunity employer. Very typical. But it got me thinking about our opportunity in this industry. Then, as I thought about it, everything came together. Indeed, this industry may be the ultimate *equal opportunity* career.

The Equal Opportunity Act came about in 1965, when President Lyndon B. Johnson signed Executive Order 11241. It was created to prohibit federal contractors from discriminating against employees on the basis of race, sex, creed, religion, color, or national origin. But for me, it has a different meaning. First, because we do not hire reps; they are independent contractors. And second, because in our case, we put extra emphasis on the word *opportunity*. For employees, it means fairness; for reps, it means an unlimited ceiling.

In this industry, having an equal opportunity does not mean everyone will take advantage of the opportunity equally. While it's a guarantee that anyone can enjoy the benefits of limitless opportunity, it still requires the effort, self-discipline, and dedication to that pursuit.

Motivational speaker and Paralympic athlete Mike Schlappi says: "The three most important words might be *take personal responsibility*." Then he added, "Or is it really four words: *take personal response ability?*" Do you have the ability to have an appropriate *response* to the opportunity in front of you?

There's an old story about two guys having a discussion about the state of society when one says to the other, "I think the biggest problems we face are ignorance and apathy." He then asks his friend, "What do you think?" The friend responds, "I don't know, and I don't care!"

I see some of that same ignorance and apathy at every meeting I attend. Here it is, an unlimited opportunity, and many choose not to take it. I am always amazed by the number of people who confuse a learning opportunity with spare time and who think multitasking will result in success.

I sat next to a rep at one conference who was checking his emails on his BlackBerry during a breakout session. He made it a point to sit in the front row of the session, but instead of paying close attention to what was being said and taking full advantage of the learning opportunity before him, he was reading and typing and sending and receiving messages. I get pretty annoyed by this kind of behavior. It is distracting to both the speaker and the attendees. I finally leaned over and asked him if he had any idea how distracting it was for a speaker to look out and see people doing that. He put his BlackBerry away and was soon gone. (By the way, this busy rep had a ribbonless badge.) Why, with all the successful reps we have speaking at these meetings, do some choose not to listen or to not even attend?

In 1978, I created the Fixed Activity Commitment (FAC) sheet, and it is still used by many agencies to this day. It is based on the idea that if we commit to doing one or two things every day for 200 working days per year, we can achieve our goals. Over time, it has become known as "One Things."[5]

The poster-size sheet contains 200 boxes representing 200 working days. The idea is to "X" out a box for every day you do your one or two controllable activities. The second part of the sheet suggests that you allocate 30 days to training and development and 30 days to vacation and quality family time. Those are all working days. Then you add in weekends, and you have a full year. The idea is to keep training days separate from other activities. The two should never cross. This allows you to dedicate yourself to lifelong learning, which includes giving your undivided attention to the speakers and avoiding the urge to step out of meetings to make calls.

First, we have to learn new information, and then we have to use what we have learned. The message of activity has never been louder or clearer. Over the past 15 to 20 years, reps have moved away from high activity in favor of "big case-itis," probably a part of the get-rich-quick economy we thought we had. We call it "big case-itis" because it is a disease. It affects the brains of many bright people who think they can do it more easily. I have 10 Rules of Life, and Rule No. 2 is that *we are all basically lazy*.

---

[5] FAC sheets are available at www.hoopis.com.

HOOPIS FIXED ACTIVITY COMMITMENT CHART

ACTIVITY X (VALIDATION + GOOD ATTITUDES) = RESULTS

Examples of fixed Activities include:

Recording Suggestions

PRODUCTION GOALS	FIXED ACTIVITIES	30 VACATION DAYS	30 TRAINING DAYS
Lives_____ New Clients_____	1_____		
Volume_____ Company Honors_____	2_____		
Premium_____ Other_____	3_____		

1	2	3	4	5	6	7	8	9	10	11	12	13	14	15	16	17	18	19	20
21	22	23	24	25	26	27	28	29	30	31	32	33	34	35	36	37	38	39	40
41	42	43	44	45	46	47	48	49	50	51	52	53	54	55	56	57	58	59	60
61	62	63	64	65	66	67	68	69	70	71	72	73	74	75	76	77	78	79	80
81	82	83	84	85	86	87	88	89	90	91	92	93	94	95	96	97	98	99	100
101	102	103	104	105	106	107	108	109	110	111	112	113	114	115	116	117	118	119	120
121	122	123	124	125	126	127	128	129	130	131	132	133	134	135	136	137	138	139	140
141	142	143	144	145	146	147	148	149	150	151	152	153	154	155	156	157	158	159	160
161	162	163	164	165	166	167	168	169	170	171	172	173	174	175	176	177	178	179	180
181	182	183	184	185	186	187	188	189	191	191	192	193	194	195	196	197	198	199	200

The Hoopis Performance Network
790 West Frontage Road
Suite 300
Northfield , IL 60093

To reorder Fixed Activity
Commitment Charts, call:
847-716-1800 or,
FAX: 847-716-1801

From the Greek root, an "itis" is an inflammation. So "case-itis" is an inflammation of our laziness.

Still, while many reps admit to having this disease, few seek treatment. The treatment is noninvasive and really only requires that you get more and better prospects and then go see them. *Is that too much to ask of someone who wants an equal and unlimited opportunity?*

The strength of our equal opportunity is not in how many *assets* we can put under management (AUM = assets under management), but instead, how many *people* we can put under management (PUM = people under management). The gift of our unlimited equal opportunity is that one life at a time, we can create a lifetime of success by adding a sufficient quantity of high-quality people to our system.

Doing this year in and year out is how we build our businesses. And a business built on a solid foundation of PUM has virtually no possibility of failure. If a business is instead built on a weak client base, it will always be vulnerable to economic and environmental fluctuations. If you are working full time at this career, you must be able to find two to four new clients per month throughout your career, not just in the early years, but every year.

So if you find it difficult to commit to high activity, start by committing to a new goal regarding lives and new clients. If we stop adding new people to our clientele, we start decreasing the chance that we can build a truly successful business. We begin the regression we talk about so often.

The leading rep at a company meeting introduced his staff of seven people. *Seven!* Now, that's a business! Following the introductions of this rep's staff, the main platform speaker made the point that the rep had a great advantage. By having seven people working at least 40 hours each, that's 280 hours of goal-achievement effort per week, and when you add in the rep's 20 hours, that's 300 hours per week of effort.

You cannot do this job alone anymore. You cannot write 100 lives or more without full-time help. The reps of old who did this were the peddlers of our business, the door-to-door salesmen. Yet I see reps all the time who are trying to build a business without adequate staff. As management guru Peter Drucker said, always have the lowest paid person capable of doing the task do the task. Find the right people so you can spend your time doing the things we selected and trained you to do — and that is to put People Under Management.

So are we an "equal opportunity" opportunity? You bet we are. But are you taking advantage of it? Make a commitment to doing one thing 200 times this year. Commit to a new client goal, and watch the growth happen. If you need to get in shape for higher activity, just commit to seeing one more person than you did the week before until you are actually seeing 15 clients face-to-face per week. *Decide once and for all to stop the mediocrity.*

Join the Turnkey Revolution

Recently, I took the time to reread *The E-Myth Revisited* by Michael Gerber, a book that has influenced my business life more than perhaps any other. I have been recommending this book to others in our industry for 20 years. One of the most important concepts in the book is something you need to be thinking about: the difference between a "trade-name franchise" and a "business-format franchise."

The book explores the question of why small businesses fail at such a high rate, while franchises succeed at such a high rate. Gerber says that despite entrepreneurs' dreams, hard work, money invested, and sacrifices, 80 percent of these small businesses fail in the first five years, and remarkably, 80 percent of the survivors fail in the next five years.[6] That means that just 4 percent of the original group survive after 10 years.

---

[6] Michael E. Gerber, *The E-Myth Revisited: Why Most Small Businesses Don't Work and What to Do About It* (New York: HarperCollins Publishers, 1995), 2.

There are several reasons, of course, but I'll keep it simple. Today's modern business-format franchise is part of the turnkey revolution in franchising. Although we are not a franchise opportunity, there is a great deal we can learn by studying the Turnkey Revolution.

In the early years of franchising, a company like Coca-Cola would award a franchise distributorship. The trade-name franchisor simply sold a franchise to some lucky person, who went about building distribution of a product, in this case, Coca-Cola. Distributors were pretty much left to figure it out for themselves. Build the network, buy the product from Coca-Cola, and the more you sold, the more you made. This was the formula used by most franchisees of the brand names we think of today.

Then along came Ray Kroc, founder of McDonald's. Kroc wanted to expand his operation but lacked the financial resources to do so. He then realized that what franchisees wanted to buy was *a business that was guaranteed to work*. And with that realization, Ray went about building a business model that even a teenager could run. This was the beginning of the move from the trade-name franchise to the business-format franchise, which was the launch pad for the Turnkey Revolution. Kroc needed to create systems and structure for every part of the business. He wanted a *system*-dependent business, not a *people*-dependent business.

Now, let's apply these concepts to our industry. For starters, we have more independence than a franchisee does, and there are practically no up-front costs to get into our business. Yes, we have to finance ourselves during the early months, and there is a lot of sweat equity, but that's about it. Compare that to the $300,000 in cash you need to get into the average franchise and more than $1.5 million needed to buy a single McDonald's franchise.

Most insurance companies have many benefits in common with a franchise. We have standardized training and products. We have brand recognition and national advertising. We have computers and a network to communicate with and operate in. And in the end, instead of a recipe for hamburgers, we have a recipe for success.

Many in our industry use the One Card System (OCS), which Al Granum created. Let's instead call it the Business Administration System, or BAS. The BAS sounds more important, and it is what a franchisee wants — a system. Regardless of the system you subscribe to, the bottom line is that we need to see at least 15 people per week face-to-face and spend at least 53 percent of our time in front of prospects and clients.

With that in mind, let's take a look at the insurance business model. One of the reasons you join a specific company is to get its secret recipe. It's not just the BAS, but it also includes some basic commitments I would require of anyone who wants an opportunity in our business. Below are some of the expectations that everyone should be willing to sign off on when they join our industry. You can succeed in our business model only if you do all of these things. To put it in McDonald's lingo, you can't just cook the hamburgers by the book; you must cook the French fries by the book too.

Before we get started trying to make our business work, everyone should agree to commit to the following:

- **Complete all of the basic training,** not just well enough to answer the questions, but well enough to really understand the information.

- **Attend all prescribed meetings,** not just the ones you think you need to, but all the meetings we think you need to.

- **Attain the professional designations of our business:** CLU, ChFC, CFP, and more.

- **Attend all company meetings,** including regional and annual meetings, because this is how your company will keep you up to date on all new products and services. There is no substitute for face-to-face learning.

- **Learn to use the products your company offers, which are needs-analysis and personal-planning tools.** Our products are the best way to help people solve many of their financial problems.

- **Build a team.** This is not a "one-man band" operation.

Now that we have agreed on the basic requirements, we can share the best practices of our top producers. We strongly recommend that you immediately implement systems that will allow you to work like they do. Here is a list of what the best do all the time:

- **They arrive at the office early. Every day.** They know that the early bird does indeed catch the worm. They also know that 90 percent of all business decisions are made by 1:00 p.m.

- **They come to work, not to play.** They work hard and play hard, but not in the same place.

- **They go home only when the work is done.**

- **They wear a suit every day.** They dress to represent their institution, not to look like their clients. The uniform is a suit, which for men includes a white shirt and a tie.

- **They are always ready.** As a friend of mine says, "My tie is my shield, and my pen is my sword."

- **They keep 15 appointments per week** and 60 face-to-face meetings per month, even if they work only 15 days.

- **They complete a needs analysis or a financial plan for everyone they meet.**

- **They spend at least 53 percent of their time in front of prospects and clients.**

- **They strive to get 500 PUM as soon as possible.** Above all else, this will get their AUM. They manage this with the BAS or OCS.

- **They work exclusively by referral** because they know their clients like the work they do for them and are always willing to tell a friend.

- **They ask for referrals at every client meeting.** They never forget, just as they never forget to breathe.

- **They never, ever take fewer than 15 fact-finders per month on new people.**

- **They keep track of activity, record it, and review it.**

- **They post and plan their activity at the conclusion of each business day.**

Welcome to our opportunity. If the inspector came by from corporate headquarters to see how well you are following the recommended guidelines, how would you do? McDonald's rescinds hundreds of franchises each year because the franchisees don't follow the chain's system. Do you have the capacity to run the business, or will it run you? Are you committed to making a better living, or are you satisfied with a mediocre one?

Write It Down

I started writing my blog, Hoopis Forum Focus, in July 2008. In sharing my thoughts with our producers, my hope was to inspire my colleagues to stretch and qualify for MDRT's Court of the Table and beyond. My great success in this regard came when one of my veteran reps said that if I committed to writing the blog each week, he would commit to making Forum, and he did! If you make a commitment to reach new heights, write it down and read it every day, and you will achieve it.

The reason that about 95 percent of all franchises succeed is because the owner commits to following the system and structure that has proven to work, time and again. The franchisee knows it would be unwise to spend all that money on a franchise and then not follow the best practices. The franchisor, wanting uniform quality and to protect its reputation, simply won't allow it to happen. So why not start today and follow the franchise model? It's a model that anyone can follow. All you have to do is to act as if you've paid $300,000 for it and see what happens. Join the Turnkey Revolution. It's a lot more fun that way!

A Culture of Greatness

Following a very special recognition dinner event in January 2011, I was inspired by the thoughts of my friend Jon Gordon, author of *Soup: A Recipe to Nourish Your Team and Culture.* I began thinking about what a special group of people we had assembled over my 35 years as managing partner. They are people in pursuit of a common goal. People serving their clients. People solving problems, not creating them. People who want the Bountiful Life and are willing to work hard to achieve it. People who want control over their future.

When asked why I think the turnover of managers in our industry is high, I have often responded that it is because too many managers build organizations they no longer want to be a part of. That is, when you don't recruit and hire people who share your values, you compromise your organization and, over time, find yourself not wanting to associate with the very people you recruited. I was always excited about our people. They are good people who do good work and bring good thoughts to mind.

> **Culture drives behavior, behavior drives habits, and habits create the future.**

Now read what Jon has to say about a culture of greatness.

In order to build a winning team and a successful organization, we must create a culture of greatness. We have that opportunity right now!

It's the most important thing we can do because culture drives behavior, behavior drives habits, and habits create the future. As the leaders at Apple say, "Culture beats strategy all day long."

When we create a culture of greatness, we create a collective mind-set in our organization that expects great things to happen — even during challenging times. We will expect our people to be their best, we will make it a priority to coach them to be their best, and most of all, we will create a work environment that fuels each person to be their best.

A culture of greatness creates an expectation that everyone in the organization be committed to excellence. It requires leaders to put the right people in the right positions where they are humble and hungry and willing to work harder than everyone else. A culture of greatness dictates that each person uses their gifts and strengths to serve the purpose and mission of our organization. It means that we don't just bring in the best people, but we also bring out the best in people.

A culture of greatness requires that we find the right people who fit into our culture. Then we will coach them, develop them, mentor them, train them, and empower them to do what they do best. As part of this process, we will develop leaders who share positive energy throughout the organization. We will also do everything possible to mitigate negativity, which sabotages the morale, performance, and success of our organization. We will deal with negativity at the cultural level so our people can spend their time focusing on their work instead of fighting the energy vampires. We will find countless ways to enhance communication, build trust, and create engaged relationships that are the foundation upon which all winning teams are built.

If creating a culture of greatness sounds like a lot of work, it is, but not as much work as dealing with the crisis, problems, and challenges associated with negative, dysfunctional, and sub-par cultures. While most organizations waste a lot of time putting out fires, we can spend our time building a great organization that rises above the competition.[7]

We can all be part of the solution and make our culture something we all want to be part of. Together, we can make it happen.

---

[7] Jon Gordon, *Soup: A Recipe to Nourish Your Team and Culture*, (Hoboken, New Jersey: John Wiley & Sons, Inc., 2010).

Why I Love the Life Insurance Business

> "Pleasure in the job puts perfection in the work."
>
> —Aristotle

At the beginning of 2010, I was in Mexico for a study group meeting. While dining at a local restaurant, I was captivated by a little girl who was dancing around on a side street. Soon, I realized that this happy little girl was with her family, and they were having dinner. I watched the story unfold.

The father was working as a security guard and watching a condo building under construction to prevent looting. The family obviously came down to join Daddy and have dinner. The makeshift dinner table was actually a huge box that contained a new dishwasher that was most likely to be installed in the house. Thus, the guard. The family gathered around the box and enjoyed their dinner. When they were done, they kissed the dad goodbye and left. The father finished cleaning up the area and sat down to continue his vigil of watching for would-be thieves.

These types of incidents always make me feel that much more grateful for the life I enjoy and the things I have been able to do — grateful that I stumbled into a career with so much opportunity. I thought about that father, working his night job at a dusty construction site and doing his best to provide for his happy little girl. Then, because of my four decades in this business, the inevitable happened, and I began to think about what would happen if that father were mugged during the night and left disabled or even dead. *What would happen to that little girl, her smile, and her dreams?* These thoughts reminded me of how thankful I am that we are able to help so many people by removing that uncertainty. And, while nothing can replace a parent, we have the ability to leave loved ones better off financially than they might have ever considered possible.

That's why I love life insurance. I like the peace of mind I get from owning it. I know that if I don't make it to age 90-plus like my dad did, I still have completed an obligation to take care of my loved ones. That makes me feel good every day. I like tax-free buildup. I like tax-free benefits. I like the fact that life insurance protects and adds to my estate. I like that it pays off debts and completes my investment plan. I like that in 2008, while the world seemed to be crashing down on us, my life insurance cash values went up. I like that I worry only about paying my premiums, and the company takes care of everything else. I like that they make the investment decisions for me, because that's not my strength. Cash-value life insurance is great property to own.

Think about this product and compare it to other types of property. Which would you rather own? It never needs polishing and never breaks or needs repair. It doesn't depreciate; in fact, it usually appreciates. You don't need a warranty because it comes with important guarantees. It has a shine to it that gets brightest when things are dark and grey in your life. It has the warmth and comfort of a cozy blanket when things go bad. It can make children smile when they otherwise would be crying. It can be a picture of a cottage on a lake for a retiree. This intangible property becomes the light of hope when people face despair. And the older it gets, the better it looks. The older we get, the more important it is. While other property wears out and must be replaced, the only wish we have as it gets older is that we have enough.

> Paint pictures for people so they understand what this remarkable product *does* — not how it *works*.

Your job as a rep is to paint these pictures for people so they understand what this remarkable product *does* — not how it *works*. Think about the last time you went into an electronics store like Best Buy. Were there any TVs on the shelf with the screen facing the wall and the backs removed so you could see how they work? No, all the TVs were probably on and facing forward so you could see what they do. It's the same for our products.

The primary reason I love life insurance is that no matter where I end up in the economic stratosphere of life, my family can stay where they are and maybe even move up a notch. It's the equivalent of what my father did for us when he insisted that we get a college education. He knew that if we had that education, we could move up in the economic stratosphere. In today's world, doing that seems more difficult than ever, but life insurance does do that. It can do things no other product that I know of can do. *It can transcend layers of the economic stratosphere!*

As I've noted, I was born into a middle-class family. My parents worked hard, taught us how to work hard, and instilled pride and integrity in us. They taught us the three Rs: respect, responsibility, and resourcefulness.

We did not have a family car, only the delivery truck we used for the grocery store. I didn't know anything about country clubs, and I never rode in a Mercedes. When I saw the life insurance business as a college intern, I immediately knew I could have an unlimited opportunity. *I knew that the life insurance business could be the funding vehicle for everything else I wanted to do in my life.* And I soon learned that, with hard work and dedication, as well as ownership of adequate cash-value life insurance, I could do today for my family what my father did so lovingly for his: move us up in the economic stratosphere!

How I Discovered Life Insurance

When I was studying to become an accountant at the University of Rhode Island in 1968, selling life insurance was the furthest thing from my mind. But I have always believed in serendipity, and that's what happened. In my auditing class in the spring of 1968, we studied, of all things, life insurance as an asset on a balance sheet. I thought life insurance as an asset? I really don't know anything about this stuff, do I? It was just weeks later when I found myself in the university's placement office looking for a part-time job so I could take a summer school class and graduate on time that it happened. There it was: an ad that read, "Sell life insurance part time." This was before internships were a big thing, but that's what it turned out to be. Well, long story short, in only 10 weeks, I learned to sell and built up my résumé. I learned that life insurance is the greatest product a person can buy, and the greatest career a person can have is to sell it.

They say that *first, you get in the life insurance business, and then the life insurance business gets in you.* That was true for me. I came into the business because I found out that I loved the thrill of making a sale. The independence appealed to me because I knew I could manage my own time. I didn't want a boss, and I had always planned to go out on my own as an accountant. I also liked it because I realized right away that a person who worked hard could make a lot of money. I liked that a lot!

Soon, however, I realized that this business was not just about making money; instead, I learned that what we do makes a difference in the lives of those we help. The sense of responsibility hit me. *I was making a difference, not just making a living!*

One of my first sales was a very small policy to a neighbor friend, Mary, who most likely just wanted to help me out. She had known me since my family moved into our house on my fifth birthday. Within a year, Mary died. I cannot tell you, even today, the impact that had on me. You see, the day she died, her brother, who was also a neighbor and friend, called and asked how much life insurance she had. He and his family were planning her funeral. I remember thinking, imagine that — the dignity and style of her funeral could be determined by the amount of insurance I sold her. And then, incredibly, the next day, the funeral director called me personally to verify that the money to pay for the funeral was indeed coming. *That's when the life insurance business got in me!*

So while I have always been a leader in pursuing the financial security model of planning that we follow today, I have also always believed that life insurance comes first. It is the foundation upon which all financial security is built.

September Is Life Insurance Awareness Month

The Life and Health Insurance Foundation for Education (LIFE) is a non-profit organization dedicated to helping consumers make smart insurance decisions to safeguard their families' financial futures. Its goal is to help consumers better understand these products and where they fit within their overall financial plans. LIFE also reminds people of the important role that insurance professionals perform in helping families, businesses, and individuals find the insurance products that best fit their needs.

LIFE designates every September as Life Insurance Awareness Month. This is an important event because millions of Americans need to be reminded about this essential product. With all the competition for con-sumers' money these days, it is easy to see how life insurance can slip to the back burner. It is our job to keep moving it to the front burner.

LIFE makes this statement in its advertising: "*A financial plan without life insurance is nothing more than an investment plan that dies when you do.*" And now that the typical investment plan has not only failed but has been set back, life insurance is even more important. Here's the prob-lem: Life insurance is something people just don't like to think about. In fact, 93 percent of Americans believe that life insurance is something most people need, yet some 70 million adult Americans have no life insurance at all. Seventy million! Add to that those who have coverage that equals just four times their income. Most experts say you need life insurance totaling at least 10 to 12 times your income.

Why is there such a gap between what people know they should do and what they actually do? A national survey shows that people who consider life insurance a necessity will do just about anything else than take steps to get it. For example, 47 percent of adult Americans say they would prefer to go to the motor vehicle office to renew their driver's license than investigate their insurance needs. Can you believe that? One in five say they would rather have a root canal. And 15 percent say they would rather babysit sextuplets. Another 11 percent say they would rather get stuck on a New York City subway without air conditioning in August!

Fortunately, there is resurgence in the workhorse product of life insurance. As Joe Belth, professor of insurance at Indiana University, said many years ago, the rep serves the anti-procrastination function. Our job is to help people take a look at their needs and take action. Nearly 50 million families have said they think they need more coverage. It's up to you to find them.

That's why I always suggest that reps worry more about getting in front of people and less about what they are going to say when they get there. I have said for years that it is pretty remarkable that reps get one out of two people they call to agree to an appointment. This number was the same when I came into the business 44 years ago. And our latest training class averaged one out of two.

Why? Because our own mortality is already on everyone's mind, and your call awakens the awareness of their need to protect their families. When you do meet them, the only sale that has to be made is them liking and trusting you. That's it. Few people buy all they need, and the rest is a budget discussion. *Tell your prospects to stop procrastinating and instead start saving money and protecting the ones they love.*

> Worry more about getting in front of people and less about what you are going to say when you get there. When you meet them, the only sale that has to be made is them liking and trusting you.

Life Insurance Is for the People Who Must Go on Living: True Stories

Several years ago, in the LIFE Foundation's infancy, I was asked to serve on its board of directors. It was a great experience for me, the life insurance guy, because I believe in the work LIFE does to increase people's awareness about their need for life insurance.

As a member of the board of directors, I was asked to serve as a judge for the organization's LIFE's Lessons Scholarship Awards. They asked students to submit essays describing the effect that owning or not owning life insurance had on their lives following the loss of one parent. Judging those essays was much tougher than one might think. I had to read 35 stories of how life insurance could have made a huge difference in the lives of these kids, but woefully, in most cases, it did not because not enough (sometimes not any) life insurance had been sold or was in force.

I can still recall the sadness of those nights, my eyes welling with tears as I read these heartbreaking stories, thinking about how much better things could have been for 35 families if only one of us had gotten there in time, if one of us had gotten there with the conviction to take a stand and tell these people what they should do, to tell them to make life insurance a priority in their lives, right along with food, clothing, and shelter. Without life insurance, the most basic human needs can go unmet after the loss of a parent.

One of the LIFE Foundation slogans is, "Life insurance isn't for the people who die. It's for the people who live." Life insurance is for the kids who want to stay in the homes they were living in before their father died. It's for the mother who would like to stay home and raise her children as a single parent instead of finding a job. It's to fulfill a parent's dream about a college education for her children so they can pursue greater opportunities in life. It's so a parent can still take care of his family even after he has left this world. In other words, life insurance is for the people who must go on living! The stories these young people wrote about their lives exemplified this theme better than anything else I can convey.

Here are a few lines from the stories I read from children who lost a parent. Each is a testament to how life insurance could have or did make a difference in their lives. I will leave it to you to imagine what they must have been going through. For me, the hardest part about reading these stories was the tone of anger that came through in some stories because while they loved the deceased parent, many wondered why and how their parents could have made such a poor decision to forgo life insurance.

Here is one such comment from a 19-year-old male whose father died when the boy was just 15 years old. *"I have reasons not to miss my dad. He did a pretty bad job providing for us and didn't have the foresight to write a will or buy life insurance."*

Another said, *"If my dad's life insurance policy had been greater and the idea of college tuition taken into consideration, the stress and unknowns my family faces today would be far less."*

Yet another student wrote of his father, *"His passing has put Mom and me through an abundance of changes and sacrifices. The funeral expenses alone were a bit much for my mom to handle alone. The family members had to donate funds to help pay for basic funeral expenses, due to lack of sufficient life insurance. … I am almost at the end of my senior year in high school. My mother and I frequently have discussions about where I want to attend college and how I will be able to attend. I see the stress and worry on my mother's face as we discuss college plans. She will always say, 'I wish I could have planned better for this.' She could have!"*

Another young person said, *"If we would have had more sufficient life insurance or had my dad been alive, I would have been able to choose a college more openly and not worry as much about the financial burden it will put on my family."*

And here is the perspective of an 18-year-old male who was 12 years old when his dad died: *"That lack of adequate life insurance is what truly sent us into a tailspin. The consequences of my father's actions have been earth-shattering. My once-proud mother has been reduced to working a menial job, and we've had to rent a room in our house to boarders. My father taught me so much in life; he was my greatest teacher. Unfortunately, the most important lesson I learned from my father, he never knew he taught me. I've learned that it is extremely important to take care of your family when you are gone and no longer able to provide for them. The greatest, most loving, and unselfish gift my father could have left was life insurance."*

Then there was this one, sad, but I am sure you will agree, different. It was written by a 17-year-old boy who was just nine when his father died: *"My whole world fell apart. My Dad was my best friend. He taught me to live life fully and to love all people. Before he died, he said it was all right to cry for him for a little while, but then to live life. Mom did not work. She devoted her life to me. My father was wise to have life insurance and health insurance and his family home so that he was able to provide for us even after his death."*

Now, that's a much happier ending.

And finally, read what this 20-year-old male had to say about his father, who died when the boy was 12. As you read it, I want you to decide if this is what you would like your kids to say. And if this is what your clients would want their children to say?

"Everything I have accomplished in life, I have done so because of him. He taught me to be strong, never to give up. He taught me to work hard for what I wanted, as he had worked hard for his family. Just as importantly, he, knowing what might come, made preparations to protect his beloved family. Though my mother always worked, she alone could never have afforded to send her three children to college. My father provided

for us even after he died. The money we could get from his well-prepared insurance plan has gotten both my brothers and soon myself through college and allowed my mother to keep the house she loved, where they had shared so many memories. My father was a scholar, and he knew that one must prepare for what could be. He knew that life could be hard, and if it were not for the measures he put in place to protect us, we could never have come so far."

By now you should be able to understand why I am a self-proclaimed "life insurance guy." I hope that the life insurance business gets in you. What greater calling can there be but to provide for kids like these? It is our job, in every single appointment we are in, to represent these children. Let's represent the ones who have written these essays and others like them so that they will not have to struggle. Life insurance, that simple document you deliver to your client, can be the hero in stories like these. It is an injustice for parents to provide a better life for their families while they are living than after they die.

If You Knew as Much about Life Insurance as I Do, You'd Buy as Much as I Have

I inherited a rep in my agency when I took over in 1977. He was a poor producer with a poor attitude toward growth. He was not my favorite rep to work with. In a meeting with him, back in the days when I thought I could save everyone, he told me that things weren't very good at home. He had traveled to Florida to move his father back to Michigan so he could put him in a state-run nursing home. When I asked why he did that, his response was, "Well, my father is destitute!" Wow, what a word, "destitute." I thought, *personally, I would be down to my last dollar before I would ever describe my father as destitute.*

Shortly after that, I decided to put him out of his misery and issued him a termination notice. I cannot work with people who care so little, who *do* so little, and, in my opinion, have no pride.

In a discussion in his final meeting, I asked how much insurance he owned. To my horror, he replied $200,000, and it was term. That's not much, even by 1978 standards. I learned a valuable lesson: You have to own it to sell it. Otherwise known as practicing what you preach, or walking the talk.

So here's a question (be honest): How much life insurance do you own? Every day we ask people to sacrifice something else that they could buy today to instead buy our product, which will protect their future in many different ways. Are you proud of your program?

I used to tell my clients and prospects, "If you knew as much about life insurance as I do, you would own as much as I do." Many, of course, asked how much I owned and why. To this day, my payment to my life insurance company is still my biggest budget item. (And I still wish I had bought even more when I was younger. Oh, how I hate admitting that!)

How Much You Should Sell

Here is the rule of thumb: You should sell each month in premium what you pay annually in premium on your own life. In other words, each year, you should sell 10 to 12 times what you own. If you are doing more, it's usually because you are still at the "running scared" stage. If you are doing less, you are entering the "I don't care" stage. Neither is good.

Evaluate how much you are paying on *your* life, not others' lives, and do the math. Qualifying as a Court of the Table producer requires an annual premium on yourself of approximately $4,000 per month. Are you there yet? If you can't buy it at half price, how can you expect others to pay full price? This is the biggest test of your sense of mission and purpose to the business. Then once you own it, all you have to do is use the magic statement, "If you knew as much about life insurance as I do, you would own as much as I do."

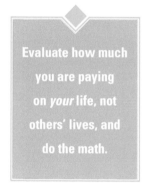

Evaluate how much you are paying on *your* life, not others' lives, and do the math.

The Bountiful Life

I attended my first Million Dollar Round Table (MDRT) meeting back in 1971. One of the speakers was a minister who told a real-life story about how life insurance helped him raise the orphaned children of his son and daughter-in-law who had been killed in an automobile crash. In closing his presentation, he said, "As a minister, I have sat on many a death bed, and there are two things I have never heard a dying man say: One, 'I have too much life insurance,' and two, 'I spent too much time with my family.'" This is the essence of what I call the Bountiful Life — doing more good in less time so that you can spend more time with your family and have the money to enjoy those things that are most important to you.

Setting an Example for Our Children

In 2008, I watched an up-close and personal segment on gold medal winner Michael Phelps. At that time, he had won 16 Olympic medals — six gold and two bronze in Athens in 2004 and eight gold in Beijing in 2008 — becoming the most successful athlete at both of these Olympic Games. He was asked how he could possibly work so hard training for his sport, swimming. He replied that he had a great role model in his mother. She was a single parent raising three kids, holding down two jobs, and studying for her master's degree. She never complained, and she seemed to always be there for him and his siblings.

In 2008, sports marketing experts and Michael's agent projected that he will earn $100 million during his lifetime, largely as a result of endorsements. Do you think he did all that training for the money, or did he do it because he was driven? And perhaps so that he would never have to say, "My mother is destitute" like my former rep said of his father? You may be lucky, like me, to have had parents who demonstrated a great work ethic. Or perhaps you didn't. But remember, either way, what you do will set an example for your children.

Life Insurance Weathers Economic Storms

When the going gets tough, the tough get going. That ought to be the mantra of every organization. In my 44 years in the business, I have been through several recessions, and I have always found that our business is a bit recession-proof. What you read about now are people hoarding cash. What better place for them to put it than with your company?

My age change occurred on November 14, 2008. That also happened to be the anniversary of several of my policies, ones I seldom think about until the annual statement arrives in the mail. With the market gyrating unpredictably every day in the throes of the recession, looking at those cash values and realizing that all I had to do to hold on to them was to continue to pay the premiums was very satisfying, to say the least. Never having to worry about market conditions, never having a sleepless night, never having to worry about financial independence, just by paying a premium. Pretty amazing.

I do not profess to be an economist or a financial guru. Instead, I like to think about how much better off I am because I am in the financial security business. I think it's important for every rep to take this opportunity to reflect on their business and on their clients' situations.

While I have watched some of the swings in the market in disbelief and read stories of attributed suicides, I haven't personally experienced any sleepless nights. Over the years, as many know, I have chosen to make my payment to my company the biggest single check I write each month. I was encouraged to do this as a young rep by my mentor, Israel Franklin, a 50-year 5L achiever (five lives issued for 600 consecutive months). For some reason, it made sense to me. Thus, every time I decided to buy a bigger home, I had to decide to increase my insurance program. Simple! Some people use 5 percent or 10 percent of their income as a guideline, but I found this to be better for me. And while this is not sexy, it has been very secure. It is comforting to know that I do not have to check my statement each morning to see how I have done.

How is your personal situation? And as you look at your clients, do you have the feeling that they, too, can sleep better at night because of you?

During the economic downturn, I had several conversations regarding the hard work needed to keep clients sane. How many of those clients have more than $1 million or $2 million in cash value? And if they did, would they be feeling better now? How many fought your recommendation to buy more life insurance because they wanted to put more in the stock market and now regret it? How many should you have led to a better place?

People are reassured and take comfort in knowing that a sound financial plan is in place. Financial security begins with taking the risk out of life. As we work on our business models, it is imperative that we look at the concept of a plan that includes life insurance.

We all know that while the investment business can be fun on the way up, it's a challenge on the way down. It's easy to smile when the assets are rolling in, the markets are brisk, and the bull is running. But when the bear comes out, it is hard work, sometimes with discouraging results. If you choose to run a balanced practice, great. Keep it up. If you are managing assets without having a strong risk-side discussion, take note: People will not forget this economic period for a long time to come, perhaps not even in the lifetimes of the youngest of you. So craft your value proposition now.

The people we work with best are those who are willing to face the personal responsibilities they have to protect their families and loved ones. Take this approach going forward, and you will find greater satisfaction in your business. If your client has $1 million or more invested with you, would it make sense for 5 percent to 10 percent of that to be in good, old-fashioned life insurance? Test the boundaries of conversation with your clients about the benefits of including life insurance in their portfolios.

Courage and Belief Are Necessary in Our Business Today

We are living in interesting times. Consumer confidence is at an all-time low. People are concerned about keeping their jobs. They're reassessing their priorities and making new decisions about what is important in life. But it is in times like these that I believe we can thrive. People are trying not to spend. Luxuries are no longer considered necessities. This is an important first step in setting a new course for America. Just as the Great Depression strongly impacted our grandparents and great-grandparents, this recession will leave an indelible mark on those living today. The term "Depression-era mentality" was coined during the Great Depression. It referred to knowing what it's like not to have the staples of life. It was about making sacrifices to find work to protect your family.

The challenge now is to convince people that when they buy our products, they are not spending, they are saving and protecting. Some may have suffered losses, leaving them less likely to self-insure against death, disability, and the problems associated with the need for long-term care. Now is your opportunity to tell the story of personal responsibility. Now is the time to reshape the thinking of your clients and prospects around sound goals, retirement planning, and financial security. Do not shirk this duty.

What it really takes to be successful in this business is a concept that was first taught to me by Dr. Don Clifton, a psychologist and professor from the University of Nebraska. Don specialized in studying the various components of talent in people. He assessed 14 characteristics found in successful people. All 14 characteristics did not need to be *strong* in a person for him or her to be considered successful, but each one at least needed to be present. There were two that he felt were a must for people in our business: courage and belief.

Courage

Don defined courage as the ability to increase persistence in the face of resistance. This is a key component for those in our industry. When people tell us no, how do we respond? What courageous activities have you attempted? Are you still waiting to call Mr. Big? Have you been afraid to ask for a referral to a client's boss?

Courage can be learned. And if we do the things we fear, the death of fear is certain. Another way to create courage while quashing fear is to increase your knowledge. Take advantage of every opportunity to learn. Conduct a learning inventory each month. What have you learned this month that you did not know last month? After 10 years as a rep, will you be a rep with 10 years of growth and experience, or will you be a rep with a year of experience 10 times? Only you can control this.

Belief — In Your Product and Service, in the Process, and in Yourself

There are three components to belief:

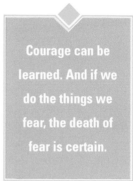

Courage can be learned. And if we do the things we fear, the death of fear is certain.

First, there's belief in *your product and service.* Do you believe in what you are doing? Are you using the planning tools provided by your company? Would *you* be happy to have you as your representative? How much of the product that you sell do you own? Are you proud of your program? Will it do the job it needs to do for you to feel good about it?

Second, there is belief in *the process.* Do you follow the process as explained in the One Card System (or whichever system you use to run your business)? It might be time to read the book again.[8] Do you make it a practice to call every client each year for a checkup? Are you sure you are taking good care of them, as promised?

Finally, there is belief in *self.* How is your self-image and self-esteem? Again, knowledge goes a long way in helping you feel better about yourself. Another way to increase self-esteem is to make a commitment and keep it. The feeling of accomplishment is a great one. Sell more lives. The validation that comes when a person writes that check and implicitly says, "I trust you, and you are my advisor" is enormous.

This is why I believe reps write lives in bunches. You know when you seem to be on a roll? That's the confidence that comes with closing sales, and when you get in front of the next prospect, you are energized and enthusiastic. As my mother always said, "The best way to increase your face value is to smile."

Every morning, keep courage and belief in your mind, and ask yourself, "What will I do today to demonstrate my courage? And how will I reinforce my belief in what I do and who I am?"

No More Mr. Nice Guy

Have you ever wondered why the last month of the fiscal year (June for many) and the month that marks the end of the calendar year (December) are always your best two months? For many, it's the realization that half

---

[8]   O. Alfred Granum, CLU; Barry Alberstein, MBA, Ph.D.; and Delia Alberstein, CLU ChFC, *Building a Financial Services Clientele: The Ultimate Guide to the One Card System,* 11th Edition (The National Underwriter Company, 2012).

a year or an entire year has slipped by, and they want to rally to save face and make up for lost time. But for great reps, the reason goes much deeper than that. It's due to a phenomenon I call "no more Mr. Nice Guy," and it applies to women, too.

Reps tend to work at optimum speed as deadlines approach. Whether it's the end of the fiscal year, the end of the calendar year, the end of a contest period, or just before a rep leaves on vacation, their capacity to get things done seems to multiply and can even quadruple. This is because of their increased focus and intensity. We know people procrastinate, and, during normal periods, we always have tomorrow to catch up. But when the crunch is on, we push harder for decisions and ask people to take action. I love yes, I can take a no, but I hate indecision.

So that Nice Guy who generally isn't pushy starts to push. Turns out, there's an important truth to be learned here. *People like to be told what to do, and they feel better about themselves when they take action and do the things they should do to meet their responsibilities.*

> People like to be told what to do, and they feel better about themselves when they take action to meet their responsibilities.

I first noticed this phenomenon many years ago. The year was coming to an end, and I began seeing apps pour in from a couple of guys who had been slow to close on business. They would always have cases ready to close but wouldn't actually close until the prospect gave them the green light. They never wanted to be the quintessential pushy salesperson. There were no hard closes for them. They were perfect gentlemen who abided their mothers' rule that "It's rude to ask."

Then it hit me. These were nice guys! They wanted to be polite, respectful, and understanding. If a client said he wanted to think it over, that was fine with them because they wanted the clients to know they were nice guys.

Why do people have this mindset? Sometimes it's the tapes they play in their mind about their own perception of what they do. Sometimes it's something someone else accused them of or made them believe. But in the end, it has transposed their definition of what a nice guy is and does.

Then it happened. One of these nice guys got a call from the wife of a prospect. She told the rep that her husband had been killed in a crash. She knew that the rep and her husband had met several times, and she wanted to know what her husband had purchased. She was hoping it was substantial. She had two young children, one more on the way, and a home she couldn't afford by herself. She was a stay-at-home mom who needed more than ever to stay at home.

Mr. Nice Guy was devastated. He told the widow that while her husband had recognized his need for life insurance, he had said he was still doing some thinking. He just wasn't sure what to buy.

The rep didn't want to push his client, and now it was too late.

The truth is that if you are *really* a nice guy, you get the insurance in force. You get the company on the hook. That's *your* role, not the widow's. If you know there is a real need, it is your job to take a position. Get the prospect to make a decision, one way or the other.

So what really happens in June and December is that reps ignore the negative feelings and thoughts they have and push Mr. Nice Guy aside while they reach their goals. This is wrong. It shouldn't be about your goals; it should be about your clients' needs. Understand that the *real* Mr. Nice Guy is the guy who gets the right insurance in force for the right reason, 12 months a year. You have to learn to recognize these false feelings of pushiness and realize that you haven't helped a family or a business until you get them to face their responsibilities. Remember, Mr. Nice Guy sells insurance.

Life Insurance Is Not Dead

Just a few years ago, a headline might have read, "Life Insurance Is Dead." A superhero attitude permeated our society, making people feel like they were never going to die and that they were all financial geniuses who would make their fortunes sitting in their homes, waiting for the value of their investments to go up. What a difference a few years can make.

Now we know conclusively that if you don't die before age 65, you will die after age 65. Imagine that. No one gets out alive! So watch the headlines. They can be misleading, if not entertaining. I have a few favorites:

"Killer Sentenced to Die for Second Time in Ten Years"

"Prostitutes Appeal to the Pope"

"Miners Refuse to Work After Death"

You also have to be careful about people's predictions. Going back a few years, I remember when someone said that the VCR would put movie theaters out of business and that Indian and riverboat casinos would turn Vegas into a ghost town. Instead movie complexes can have up to 30-plus theaters, and Las Vegas has doubled in size since the first riverboat casino set sail. I don't think either of those scenarios has happened, do you?

Another prediction, one closer to home, forecasted that Internet sales would eliminate most if not all insurance agents. It turns out that fewer than 2 percent of sales are made online, and those companies that do sell life insurance online struggle to stay in business. Life insurance isn't dead. In fact, in today's environment, it's alive and kicking. It has had a resurgence for what it was and always has been: peace of mind. It is the vehicle to save and to protect the people we love most. It is the proven way for people to ensure that they and their loved ones will be all right.

An Enormous Market Waiting for Your Call

According to LIMRA, U.S. ownership of life insurance is at an all-time low. One reason is that we have fewer people selling life insurance these days. Compliance and continuing education have done a good job of knocking out thousands of poorly qualified and questionable reps. In addition, some companies have abandoned their distribution systems because they were too expensive to build. But the other side of that equation is that we have an enormous opportunity ahead of us. LIMRA research reveals that almost one-third of U.S. households, some 35 million, don't have any life insurance at all.

One family in four relies solely on employer-sponsored life insurance, a risky proposition. With unemployment at 7 percent,[9] consider how many people have lost their coverage through their employer. Half of all U.S. households, 58 million families, readily admit they currently don't have adequate life insurance coverage. It's the highest number ever. Forty percent say the major reason for not buying is that they are paying off debt or saving for retirement. LIMRA also says that seven out of 10 families would have trouble paying their bills if the primary wage earner died unexpectedly. Without the safety net of life insurance, most families would have limited time before their savings ran out. Of families with children under age 18, four in 10 say they would immediately have trouble meeting everyday expenses if the primary wage earner were to die.

Even affluent households lack sufficient life insurance, with one-third saying they do not have enough coverage. These are people who think six times their income is sufficient, yet we know that is not enough. LIMRA research also tells us that consumers are looking for trusted advisors, a referral from a family member or friend. One in four households does not know how to reach its financial goals.

[9] U.S. Department of Labor, Bureau of Labor Statistics. http://data.bls.gov/timeseries/LNS14000000.

It's up to you. You can look out your window and see 8 million people who need your help, or you can sit there and say you have no one to call. You can persist in getting your clients to introduce you to their friends and relatives, or you can continue to tell yourself that people don't give referrals.

There is an enormous market waiting for you to call. So stop making excuses. Instead, make more calls. Easy jobs still don't pay much. If you are seeing fewer than 15 people per week, you have an easy job. If you are like the best I know, and you keep 60-plus appointments per month, you are making a great living, and you are enjoying the Bountiful Life. The choice is yours.

> Seven out of 10 families would have trouble paying their bills if the primary wage earner died unexpectedly.

Financial Reps Are Like Baseball Umpires

I have always suggested that the job of the financial representative is to act like the umpire in baseball. Periodically, during a typical game, the umpire stops the game, positions himself over home plate, bends over, takes out his little whisk broom, and cleans the dust and dirt off home plate. That allows the pitcher, the batter, and the umpire himself to better see the target. This is what I suggest a rep do when he or she meets with a client, whether it is for the first time or for an annual review. We stop the game, clear the dust, dirt, and distractions, and get the client to focus on the target: financial security for the client's family and the peace of mind that only proper planning can bring.

In our brief meetings, fact-finding sessions, and annual reviews, we ask our prospects and clients to look at some things that are easily covered up or overlooked in the course of day-to-day living. It is in that brief period of time that we get to ask the important questions about the family's aspirations and dreams — their goals plus their wish list. We talk about the things that can go wrong, the foul balls of life. We ask them to take action before they strike out. If we are unsuccessful, the dust and dirt of daily life will quickly cover home plate again, and the client probably will not consider these issues again until the next rep gets in and brushes off home plate. *If we are successful, we can change the outcome of any game, whether it goes to extra innings or not.*

It's time to ask more people to take a "time-out" in the game of life. Get out your whisk broom, and get them to take a good look at their life issues before the dust and dirt settle and they run out of innings.

Why People Don't Own Life Insurance: "Every Excuse in the Book"

Despite all the bad news about our economy over the past few years, there is some good news. According to LIMRA research, about 48 million U.S. heads of household believe they need more life insurance.

So why aren't most prospects calling you?

LIMRA decided to ask the same question of a large group of consumers. Their conclusion, presented in the report "Every Excuse in the Book," was that this group would not be easy to reach unless the industry made some fundamental changes.

It's Unpleasant and Stressful to Discuss Mortality

So what has happened in the past that has consumers holding back even when they say they need more coverage? For one thing, consumers report that the topic is unpleasant and stressful. One consumer said, "It's a boring subject, morbid to think about needing it, and it's scary overall." The discomfort they envision when thinking of going through the process stops them from even getting started.

The Decisions Are Overwhelming

Just thinking about the decisions to buy life insurance can be overwhelming. It can feel too complicated and confusing. One consumer said, "It is overwhelming and complicated, and you are not sure you can get through the maze. It's like you are lost forever."

It is eye-opening to discover the basic concepts the underinsured do not understand about life insurance. Perhaps even more remarkable is that consumers with household incomes of $100,000 or higher lack basic knowledge about life insurance products. When given the opportunity to ask questions about life insurance, here are some of the questions people need answers to:

- What do you need life insurance for?
- What are the different types of life insurance available?
- How much life insurance do we need? What is the average?
- At what age should I think about buying?
- How is it paid out?

■ Is there a life policy that doesn't get more expensive each year?

Think about your own client presentation. Be sure your presentation helps provide the answers to these common and predictable questions.

People Procrastinate

Of course, some did mention procrastination as a problem. Some consumers procrastinate because they feel they are too busy and don't have the time to go through the odious task of buying life insurance, while others are waiting for someone to approach them. One consumer said, "I know I need it but think I will do it tomorrow."

People Distrust the Distribution System

Others say they don't trust the distribution system, and they prefer face-to-face contact. They question whether the representative will take the time to understand their needs and whether the agent has their best interest in mind. One young husband said, "I felt they (reps) are not always looking out for the best product for me, but looking out for the best product for them to sell me." And they don't like getting hammered for hours on end. Instead, people want a trusted advisor who connects with them on a regular basis. They want someone to walk them through the choices.

People Can't Find a Trusted Advisor

Unfortunately, most consumers haven't seen or heard from an agent in years. One said, "I had a good insurance guy but haven't seen the guy in 15 years. Trust is so vital to the life insurance process and the relationships you establish and maintain that consumers are more likely to buy if the rep is recommended by someone who the consumer trusts or if the individual already has a relationship with the sales representative. Participants said it was difficult to find a trusted advisor and that they might get started buying life insurance if "[they] could find someone [they] trust or get a referral from a close personal friend or financial advisor."

> They want you to build a relationship, and you cannot do that in 15 minutes. They want you to be patient and listen to their needs before you try to sell them what they need.

In addition to those excuses, other consumers said they didn't know we still sold life insurance. Some are confused by advertising. Others want a review of what they have bought. They don't feel we listen well. One participant said, "If I tell you what I am looking for, start there." They want you to build a relationship, and you cannot do that in 15 minutes. They want you to be patient and listen to their needs before you try to sell them what they need. And don't try to scare them or use guilt tactics.

What They Do Want

Consumers want the life insurance buying process to be easy and pain-free. They want straight talk, and they want you to use layman's terms, not industry terminology or jargon. They want a short meeting with an agent who will listen to them and talk about what they need and not what an agent wants to sell them. They're busy. Meetings shouldn't last longer than one hour. And they want to know three things:

- What is it?
- What will I get?
- What will I pay?

Answer those questions for them without exerting pressure, be someone they can trust, and understand their situation. You can build trust by showing you are sincerely interested in them, by showing that you understand what they need, and by taking the time to build a relationship with them and being willing to educate them.

So there you have it, the keys to the kingdom. Forty-eight million households say they need more life insurance coverage, and now you know how to sell to them.

My advice:

- Read this section of the book several times.
- Make it the topic of your next study group meeting.
- Work on making the process more pleasant.
- Practice the teaching skills.
- Don't assume that prospects know much about the product.
- Work from an agenda that lists topics and the time needed to cover each so that you can get the job done in one hour.
- Be brief. Ask the prospect how much time they have to spend. Agree to stay in touch, and then do so.
- Work on smiling and being positive in every meeting.

- Explain to current clients that their friends and loved ones actually are waiting for you to refer them.

Stop claiming there is no one to sell to! There are people out there who need you. Find them. Share this LIMRA study with every person you meet with. And by all means, stay in touch with your clients.

If life insurance has gotten into you, then you will love insurance as much as I do, own a lot of it, and encourage your clients to protect their families with the greatest product they could ever buy.

The Three I's: Independence, Impact, and Income

Some of the people who are reading this chapter work "on purpose," and their efforts bring tears to my eyes. You are the ones who made this career possible for me, and for that I am grateful.

Former managing partner Marty Polhemus, a great friend of mine from Spokane, Washington, was an inspiration to so many. He used to say, "This is a tough business, but for the right person, it's the closest thing to heaven on Earth that there is!"

That really is true. We have independence, impact, and income, three very important benefits to those of us who work hard to stay in the business. But we need to work on these things every day. It's like eating: It can't be done once and for all. It must be done daily, and several times a day at that.

There is an old American saying, "Business is like a car; it will not run by itself except downhill." How is your business running? Are you in the driver's seat? Showing up at the office every day does not make you a successful rep any more than standing in a garage makes you a car. You have to do something while you are there.

Independence is the key to achieving impact and income. Independence is often interpreted as *flexibility*. Instead, it needs to be interpreted as *opportunity*. Reps who think that because they are in business for themselves they can come and go as they please are sure to stumble and fail. Flexibility is a killer. We are all basically lazy (Hoopis Rule No. 2), and flexibility enables laziness. You won't get ahead in life unless you exert a superior effort.

Impact follows independence. When we seize the opportunity that our business offers, the impact we can have is incredible. Individuals, families, companies, and even communities benefit from the work we do. Families stay together; children are able to remain in their homes and continue in their schools; businesses survive the loss of owners and key people; the impact of loss and tragedy on the community is lessened.

Income then follows as the by-product of great achievement, and so the circle of success is completed. This is how we reach the Bountiful Life.

I intentionally placed the three benefits in order: independence, impact, income. If you respect the cycle, you will reap its rewards.

If we are true to ourselves, and we manage our time and purpose, good things will come. We earn what we receive, and so no thank-yous are necessary. Let me explain.

The first job I had outside of my father's grocery store was at Harvest Bread, a large bakery on the East Coast. I worked a variety of jobs, from making doughnuts to mixing dough to watching the ovens that baked the hot dog rolls. It was a good job for a kid, with lots of available overtime. I once set a record working a 27-hour shift and 78 hours in one week. (I went from regular time to double time in a week. What a thrill!) If they needed someone, I was there.

My boss, nicknamed Joe Fats, was a tough guy who walked around all day barking at people. The workers were generally afraid of this guy. Every week he would walk around the plant and personally pass out paychecks. It was his way of letting everyone know who was in charge. As he approached me each Thursday with my envelope, I would become both nervous and excited. I had been raised properly, so when he handed it to me, I said, "Thank you, Joe," to which he would bark, "Kid, if you earned it, you don't have to say thank you!"

Wow, what a lesson. Being thankful is a good thing, but the concept of *earning* was an epiphany for me. The idea of exchanging my time and talent for money was rewarding.

Then I found our business, in which time and talent are exchanged for commissions. I discovered that the better I was at solving problems for people, the more I could make. *I* determined what I was worth per hour, not Joe Fats! *I* had the advantage to earn an unlimited income if I channeled my independence into productive activities. Doing that with lots of people who need our advice has resulted in the ability to have a significant impact on the families and businesses I work with, and that has resulted in the income I desire. It's a circle of success that cannot be beat.

Money is a by-product of great achievement.

So if you earned it, be grateful, but don't say thanks. And if you are not earning it, ask why. Or, as Confucius said, "A man who stands on a hill with his mouth open will wait a long time for a roast duck to drop in."

Close your mouth and get to work. It's time to make a difference in more lives each day. Remember: Money is a by-product of great achievement.

Do What Top Advisors Do

A few years ago, my wife, Bea, and I saw a show in Las Vegas. One of the opening acts was a group called Oh What a Night.[10] They performed a tribute to Frankie Valli and the Four Seasons. It was like attending a short version of the Broadway hit *Jersey Boys*. It was a lot of fun. Bea and I were enjoying the show when she leaned over and said, "They look, sound, and act just like the Four Seasons." The exaggerated dance moves were hilarious. The choreography was perfect. The Four Seasons were known for their moves, as well as their music, and this group had it down pat.

I said to Bea, "Well, I guess if you are going to make a living imitating the Four Seasons, you had better study everything they do and do it exactly like they do it." These four guys did!

Likewise, if you want to make a living in financial services, you had better study what the stars do and do it exactly like them.

So if you want to make a living like a Top of the Table producer, you had better study everything those producers do. Each year at the MDRT meeting, we watch some of the greatest role models in the industry as they are introduced. We sit there thinking about how great it would be to be like them. We dream about the Bountiful Life and what it would mean to our families.

And then some reps get home and forget to do anything about emulating those producers. Once you return from that meeting, and others, a good question to ask yourself is, *What did I learn at the meeting that I want to implement? What am I doing differently since the meeting? What have I changed? What am I doing that I have never done before to improve my practice?*

> "The key is to keep company only with people who uplift you, whose presence calls forth your best."
>
> —Epictetus

---

[10] The performance schedule and other information about the group Oh What a Night is available at http://frankievalliandthe4seasonstribute.com/.

Here is what motivational speaker Tony Robbins said about impersonating successful people: "If you want to be successful, find someone who has achieved the results you want and copy what they do, and you'll achieve the same results." It's a lot like what that Frankie Valli tribute act Oh What a Night did when they decided to impersonate the Four Seasons.

Differentiating Characteristics of Top Reps

The top third of reps are typically six times more productive than the bottom third. Unbelievable as that may seem, we know this based on studies of reps who are between their fifth and 15th years in the career.

But just about all reps could stand to become even more successful. If you are in the lower third, don't you want to change that? If you are in the middle third, don't you want to make the adjustments that could take you to the next level? And if you are in the upper third, don't you want to fine-tune the things you do so that you can move into the top 10 percent?

Let's talk about what the best of the best are doing.

MDRT conducted a study a few years ago that looked at member productivity among its three membership levels. In 2010, MDRT reps had to make approximately $90,000 in first-year commissions (FYCs) to qualify for base membership. Membership in Court of the Table, which is three times the base, required $270,000 in FYCs. And membership in Top of the Table, which is six times the base, was $540,000 in FYCs.

The requirements for Court of the Table and Top of the Table are pretty impressive. So how do these producers excel at such high levels? It would stand to reason to think they work harder and longer than anyone else. But suppose I told you that the more they produce, the *fewer* hours they work! MDRT discovered that base members spent an average of 19 percent of their time in front of prospects and clients. Court of the Table members spent 48 percent of their time in front of prospects and clients. And Top of the Table members spent 53 percent of their time in front of prospects and clients.

So how do top insurance and financial services professionals spend that much time in front of prospects and clients? Simple. They have a lot of prospects because they never forget to ask for names. They have lots of clients. Top of the Table producers write three times the lives of the regular member. And they have staff members so they can stay out of the muck and mire of office administration.

Court of the Table members write twice the number of lives as base members; Top of the Table members write three times the number that base members do. So unless you are writing more than 100 lives per year with sufficient new clients, don't make any big plans and don't dream any big dreams because you probably will not become wealthy. The best producers build their business around the concept of "high lives productivity." Over time, they improve the quality of their prospects and their knowledge, which leads to even bigger sales. And here is the big payoff: MDRT producers reported working 58 hours per week; Court of the Table producers, 54 hours; Top of the Table producers, 51 hours. For Top of the Table qualifiers, that's up to 30 fewer hours per month and six times the production.

> Top of the Table qualifiers work up to 30 fewer hours per month and make six times the production.

We conducted a study among our reps and found similar results. We discovered that the three differentiating characteristics of our top producers are:

1. Repeat sales.

If you've been in the business for five years or longer, you know that you should be calling all of your clients regularly, introducing them to the specialists in your office who can ensure that their changing needs are being met, and keeping them up to date on changes in their programs. All too often, reps don't follow through with these important touches. I don't understand why. Reread Al Granum's book *Building a Financial Services Clientele: The Ultimate Guide to the One Card System*. For those of us in insurance and financial services, it's our bible.

2. Use of planning tools.

These include personal planning and needs analysis tools. First, do you use them? If not, why not? Too much work? Didn't learn them? These aren't reasons; they're excuses. If you are committed to achieving the Bountiful Life, you have to use these tools. There's no getting around it.

Facts directly from one home office will help you better understand why. Individuals who used the planning tools had 17 percent higher premiums than those who did not. They also had 71 percent more new clients and 29 percent higher cross-selling results. These tools are vital to your success and absolutely necessary if you want to achieve the Bountiful Life. Choose to be a problem solver, not a product pusher.

Better still? Those who were in the top quartile of users of the planning tools, meaning those doing 60 or more plans per year, did 24 percent more premium, had 128 percent more new clients, and did 44 percent more cross-selling.

These numbers speak for themselves, but just in case you aren't convinced, here are a couple more reasons to do planning for everyone you meet. LIMRA International studies indicate that doing a plan for a prospect or client puts a virtual fence around them for up to five years. In other words, when the time is right for them to buy, they will remember that you put forth the effort, and they will buy from you. That alone makes using the planning tools worth it.

3. Growth in credentials.

The statistics from The American College regarding the income differences between CLUs and non-CLUs are compelling. Then add the ChFC designation, and the difference is even greater; it more than doubles a rep's income. If you have been in this business for more than five years and haven't achieved these designations, you need to get serious about one or both this year. You are smart enough to pass the tests, but are you smart enough to take them? Exert some self-discipline. Take the classes. Study hard, and take the exams. It's that simple. The dividends will pay tenfold.

If you have been in this business for fewer than five years, model what the top producers do, and keep your activity levels high. The key to activity is to get in front of prospects and clients. Go to your company or professional association website, or visit Hoopis Performance Network (HPN) and access the resources that show how top producers build a strong practice.[11] For instance, on HPN you can watch Al Granum talk about the importance of calling every client in your files and increasing your time in the field. The video is classic Granum and a must-see.

Start with small things. Epictetus said, "Practice yourself, for heaven's sake in little things, and then proceed to greater."

I don't understand why so many people sit on the sidelines of life and let opportunity pass them by. I don't understand why they won't study the best practices and do something to improve their situation. I guess it all goes back to Rule No. 2: We are all basically lazy. But high achievers are always looking for ways to make their work easier and more enjoyable.

---

[11] Information on HPN can be found in the Resources for Lifelong Learning section beginning on p. 187.

These are the keys to the kingdom. You only need to pick them up and open the door.

Now, let's look at some good habits to get into, habits that are second nature to top advisors.

Recognize Your Team Members

Let me describe your team. It's your associate rep and your immediate staff, of course. But it is also the folks in new business, the specialists, your fellow ClientBuilder members, your director of operations and chief development officer, your managing director, and your managing partner. In other words, it's everyone, because they all know that nothing good can happen unless you are selling and serving and are happy and prosperous.

But the most important member of your team is your spouse or significant other. This is the person who sacrifices having your time and attention during a sprint period that could last eight to 10 weeks. This is the person who backs you up day in and day out, year after year, when others have come and gone. So make sure you give him or her an extra-long hug before you leave home in the morning. Of course, it's not as bad as when prehistoric man or even the pioneers headed out to hunt their prey; they could have been gone for months. And it's certainly not like the sacrifices our soldiers make when they deploy for a year or more to serve in harm's way. God bless those who serve this great country. So keep things in perspective. You can do this if you try, and it won't kill you.

Manage Your Time Wisely

To help you reach your objectives, I suggest becoming more efficient in time management than ever before.

- **Close your door.** Learn to prioritize effectively. Don't do anything but work while in the office. Stop all personal phone calls except to check in with family. Keep chat with staff or colleagues to a minimum.

- **Optimize.** Every 15 minutes, ask yourself, "What is the best use of my time right now?"

- **Prioritize.** Make a list of all open cases and prioritize them. Call them to schedule appointments as soon as possible.

- **Communicate.** Find reasons to send a note or email to your clients.

- **Look for opportunities to resell or cross-sell.** Long-term care and disability are important products, and cash-value life insurance is great for kids.

- **Set up a day in the next two weeks to prospect with your best clients.** Remember, 30 days ago, we didn't even know 80 percent of the new people we sell to each month. There is still plenty of time for new clients.

- **Make more phone calls.** And tell the reps who aren't in the game to not bother you.

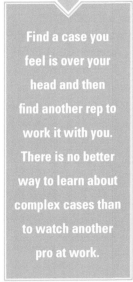

Find a case you feel is over your head and then find another rep to work it with you. There is no better way to learn about complex cases than to watch another pro at work.

Go on Joint-Work Appointments

I always advised the newest people in our organization to set up 30 joint-work appointments with 10 different reps who are doing what they would like to be doing. I ask the new reps to get this done in their first 90 days. It's the 30/10/90 formula, and it is the best way to learn what the best people in an organization are doing.

I also suggest that the new reps offer to drive the more experienced reps to the appointments so they can have more of their time, and to ask every question they can think of on the way to the appointment.

This strategy isn't just for new reps, though. I advise all veteran reps to find a case they feel is over their head and then find another rep to work it with them. There is no better way to learn about complex cases than to watch another pro at work.

You can't copy everything another person does; just look for the traits you can emulate, and over time you will create a masterpiece that is your own. But you must do this with the top reps, not the ones who haven't figured it out yet. *Amateurs teach amateurs to be amateurs.* As my friend Howard Bennell used to say, "If you want to make $100,000 per year, don't ask a person making $20,000 how to do it."

Commit to Activity, Lifelong Learning, and Prospecting

When you study top producers, you will discover that they are committed to maintaining a high level of activity, continuing their lifelong learning, and constant prospecting.

- **Top producers run their business with a high level of activity.** Top producers stay in control of their activity. They find ways to be sure activity does not slip. They are adamant about this, and it is one of the things I admire most about them. They control the situation and never let the situation control them. If they only have 15 days to work, they still keep 60 appointments. I know too many advisors who have 15 days to work and keep just 30 appointments. Remember: Peak and valley activity begets peak and valley results.

- **Top producers commit to lifelong learning.** I know I talk about this a lot, and it's because I cannot say it enough. Balancing your activity with your learning is essential to your ongoing success. Planning your learning activities should be included in your annual planning and goal-setting. You can do this effectively by taking advantage of online resources to watch some of the best and brightest in the industry with just a few clicks.[12] Your development plan should also include the in-person learning that takes place at meetings and conferences.

- **Top producers prospect all the time.** Top producers don't prospect only after the prospect becomes a client, but every time they have an opportunity to ask. They also "prospect up," asking for introductions to bosses and superiors. They expect great leads from their clients, and they are relentless in pursuing them. And when they get them, they do something with them. *They don't just shuffle the cards; they deal with them!*

You are not really making it in this business unless you are making MDRT. Study Top of the Table producers, and do what they do. They are truly inspirational.

The Importance of Lifelong Learning

Lifelong learning is the first key to success in our business, yet many advisors fail to attend company meetings to learn from the very best. Others show up, but miss important sessions because they sleep in or leave early. This is just one example of the things people do to sabotage their success. Some people are content to rationalize their complacency and mediocrity. Top producers are never complacent, and they never settle for mediocrity. You have to care more about your success than anyone else. And your actions are a reflection of your personal desire to succeed.

Founded in 1987, Hoopis University helped our advisors pursue their commitment to lifelong learning. It offered programs that helped them

---

[12] Information on HPN's Virtual Coach videos is available at www.hoopis.com.

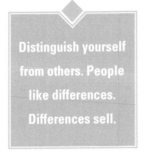

Distinguish yourself from others. People like differences. Differences sell.

improve their selling and relationship-building skills.

One of our early programs featured two of LIMRA International's training programs, facilitated by an outstanding instructor, Delores Freitag. One was called "Understanding and Adapting Your Sales Style," and the second was titled "Top Producer Mindset Differential." Both featured assessments to give attendees important personal insights. In one section, Delores discussed some research LIMRA did on behavioral economics.

Here are a few nuggets of wisdom that Delores revealed during those programs.[13]

- People like differences. Differences sell. How is what you do different? Perhaps it's your planning process. Or maybe you take down facts about a client and prepare a brief. Whatever it is, be different. Distinguish yourself from others.

- People like to know that other people have bought a product, and why.

- To be an effective communicator, use real words for real people. Make it easy for people to understand what you're offering and to see the benefits. Use plain English.

- People like rules of thumb and guidelines. For example, many people target 10 times their income as a good amount of insurance to own. Another good rule of thumb is to save 15 percent of your gross income each year.

- People like to hear and see three recommendations. Give them choices without compromising the plan.

- People think better in monthly terms than annual. Fit your products into their monthly budgets.

Continue to Learn with Video Training

The second trait that top producers share is that they have made a commitment to lifelong learning. When you start your day by tapping into a learning system, you feel enriched and empowered, and you gain a sense of accomplishment.

---

[13] This information and the two assessments are included in the *Trustworthy Selling* training program, www.hoopis.com.

Why not start each day with a short video clip that could improve a skill? You could watch a segment on prospecting before you go out on a prospecting interview. Or view a video on fact finding before you go out on a fact-finder. Or watch a segment on phoning before you do your morning dials. How about a segment on closing before going out on a closing interview? Or, before making a sales call, why not watch a segment on how life insurance has helped someone in need?

Videos are an excellent way to improve your education, knowledge, and skills all on your own. Wouldn't it be great to watch a segment on estate-planning basics to reinforce some things you have already learned but perhaps have forgotten? Listen to the words some of the best in the business use on appointments before going out on your own.

Paul Coffey is a retired professional Canadian ice hockey defenseman who played in the National Hockey League (NHL). He ranks second among NHL defensemen in career points, goals, and assists. He said, "Nobody's a natural. You work hard to get good and then work hard to get better. It's hard to stay on top." That's true in our business, too.

What are you committed to? What are you doing to get better? How do you plan to stay on top? One of the easiest ways to do this is to commit to regular online video training. There is something for everyone online — from sales skills and practice management to sales teams and motivation.

Be better. Improve yourself. Try something new to move yourself toward greater success.

Maintain High Activity

I encourage high activity because it is the only thing that I know that works on a consistent basis. Everyone wants to talk about the exceptions to the rule of high activity; I choose to accept it as rule No. 1. As Al Granum says, "High activity, even enough of the right kind, doesn't guarantee success, but without it, success is almost impossible."

In my former agency, we recognized a group called "Forum." To qualify, a rep needed to produce approximately $225,000 in FYCs. Forum producers are 100-plus lives writers. Consistent

> A lot of business is written by accident, but you have to be out where the accidents are happening.

Forum producers are typically at 100 lives by the fifth year and stay above 100 lives through their 17th year, industry wide. Seventy percent of all Forum producers make Forum by their ninth year, and 83 percent of consistent Forum producers do so by their ninth year. Forum producers write lots of lives, and they are not all big ones.

They also believe, like I do, that a lot of business is written by accident, but you have to be out where the accidents are happening. The average Forum producer writes more than 40 lives with premiums under $1,000. It's true. In fact, there are remarkably few cases over $10,000 of premium and even fewer over $25,000. The $10,000-plus lives represent just 4 percent of the total lives sold but account for 64 percent of their premium.

Forum producers are focused on high activity. They are out there seeing their clients on a regular basis. They create agendas that show planning priorities. They are consistent users of the personal planning and needs analysis tools. Top producers spend more time in front of clients and prospects. But they also spend more time golfing, more time coaching their kids' sports teams, and more time on vacation. They spend less time in the office, where their time is easily wasted, and they build a competent staff that allows them to stay out of the office doing all of the things I just mentioned.

Forum producers are dedicated people. They attend ClientBuilder meetings regularly. They are members of companywide study groups with other top producers. They believe in high accountability and do not look for places to hide. They take personal responsibility for their success. You seldom hear

Service is the rent we pay for the space we occupy on this Earth.

them blaming underwriting, new business, or the weather for a lack of productivity. MDRT producers believe, like I do, as I state in rule No. 5 of life, that "Bad things happen to all people, both good and bad, but good things tend to happen more often to good people." Top reps believe that service is the rent we pay for the space we occupy on this Earth, and they look for ways to serve in their business, spiritual, and community lives. They are more likely to help a sick child facing mortality too soon live out a fantasy than they are to play fantasy football.

These people are living the Bountiful Life.

Establish Good Habits

Here is a great poem about habits:

> I am your constant companion.
>
> I am your greatest asset or heaviest burden.
>
> I will push you up to success or down to disappointment.
>
> I am at your command.

Half the things you do might just as well be turned over to me,

For I can do them quickly, correctly, and profitably.

I am easily managed, just be firm with me.

Those who are great, I have made great.

Those who are failures, I have made failures.

I am not a machine, though I work with the precision of a

Machine and the intelligence of a person.

You can run me for profit, or you can run me for ruin.

Show me how you want it done. Educate me. Train me.

Lead me. Reward me.

And I will then ... do it automatically.

I am your servant.

Who am I?

I am a habit.

We hear a lot about the importance of habits. For example, I recommend that all reps get into the habit of working while travelling in their cars. Between the hours of 7:00 a.m. and 7:00 p.m., Monday through Friday, reps should have the radio and the music off. During this time, while driving to or from the office or appointments, they should be engaged in thought exercises. This is when they should be thinking about their goals, dreams, and aspirations, focusing on family objectives, rehearsing for the next appointment, role-playing what might happen, or thinking about how the last appointment went. All of these fall under what I call Work Orientation, or WO, the first half of WORK.

The second half of WORK is RK, Receive Knowledge. That's easy to do these days with the abundance of audio CDs and access to HPN Mobile. Listen to great speakers or autobiographies of famous people. Get inspirational messages to motivate you.

Do this three hours each day, which is the average driving time a rep does in a day, five days a week, and you will have 15 hours of think time and learning a week. That's 60 hours a month, or 720 hours per year. Eighteen 40-hour weeks of meaningful WORK, instead of just driving and daydreaming. I have done this for more than 40 years, and I guarantee you that it will have a profound effect on your professional and personal development.

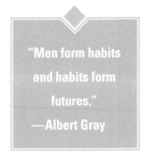

Develop Good Habits — and Then Maintain Them

"Men form habits and habits form futures."
—Albert Gray

If you study top advisors' strategies, you will see that they develop and maintain good habits.

In 1940, Albert E. N. Gray, with The Prudential Insurance Company of America who had been in the life insurance industry for 30 years, delivered a presentation to life insurance professionals titled "The Common Denominator of Success." Available as a paperback, this work has been quoted frequently for 70-plus years. One statement that resonated with me was this: "Men form habits and habits form futures."[14]

How Purpose Can Help Create Habits

Purpose is the object one strives for. Have you defined your purpose?

Over the years, I have learned to ask one simple but very important question of newer reps: "Why are you working?" A typical answer is "Because I have bills to pay." That is true; we all have bills to pay, but if that is all that gets you out of bed each morning, it won't provide the fuel necessary for extraordinary performance.

Only the *extra* in extraordinary performance will help you get what you want out of life. If you can do some *extra* ordinary things — not extraordinary but rather *extra* ordinary things, or more ordinary things than anyone else — you will achieve surprising and amazing results.

The most successful people in any occupation are not those who do things differently; they are the ones who do more of the ordinary things: more calls, more referrals, more appointments, more fact-finders, and more closes. You do not have to be *extraordinary* to be successful in this business; you just have to do *extra* ordinary things.

So if your purpose can drive habits, your habits will drive your success. Good *habits are hard to form but easy to live with, and bad habits are easy to form but hard to live with.* And, as Mr. Gray told us, *habits form futures.*

Many reps feel compelled to tie their purpose to their occupation, something like, "I help people in times of need," or "I sell peace of mind." And while this is true, it is generally not sufficient to produce *extra* ordinary activity and results. This is clear because we all sell great products, but we are not all selling at the same level.

---

[14] Albert E. N. Gray, "The Common Denominator to Success," p. 1, accessed December 11, 2013, http://www.amnesta.net/mba/thecommondenominatorofsuccess-albertengray.pdf.

This is because when it comes to human achievement, it is all about the individual. It's about what your needs are. And if you take good care of yourself, you will naturally take good care of those around you — your family, friends, and clients. Money is a by-product of great achievement. If we do a good job, we will be rewarded.

Mr. Gray also said, "Successful people do the things they don't like to do because they can accomplish the things they want to accomplish. Successful people are influenced by the desire for pleasing *results*, while failures are influenced by the desire for pleasing *methods* and are inclined to be satisfied with the results which can be obtained by doing things they like to do."[15]

This is fundamental to the key to success, and I wish more people would understand this point: The key is the *result*, not the *method*. Purpose drives us to do the things we need to do, the *extra* ordinary things.

Mr. Gray asked whether having a family to raise and children to educate was enough to motivate a person to do better. His answer? No, because "It's easier to adjust ourselves to the hardships of a poor living than it is to adjust ourselves to the hardships of making a better one. If you doubt me, just think of all the things you are willing to go without in order to avoid doing the things you don't like to do."[16]

How Urgency Can Help Us Create Habits

Motivational speaker Jim Rohn said, "Without a sense of urgency, desire loses its value." One of the most discouraging parts about my job (yes, even I have some) is that while we are almost always successful in contracting people who can sell, we discover that some are not willing to apply that ability in their daily pursuit. If you are a parent who has witnessed one of your children not using their God-given talents wisely or not living up to their potential, then you know how I feel. Ours is a wonderful relationship, but I can't do well if you don't do well.

If you are a newer rep in the business, I want you to think about having a sense of urgency that lasts for your first 10 years. As I reflect on my years in the business, I know for certain that the reps who are happiest in their careers worked the hardest in the first 10 years. Hard work is defined as the highest activity combined with the most new clients and the most lives. Do this consistently for 10 years, and your clients will take care of you after that.

[15] Gray, ibid, 3.
[16] Ibid.

That's what I mean when I say there is a price for success, and it is always paid in advance. Build that clientele quickly. Work at it every day. Make nearly everything else second to building a solid foundation for your business in the first 10 years, and you will have more free time later to spend with your family and friends. It is one of the most rewarding sacrifices you will ever make. Let's call it the "Fast 10, Fun 20." Lots of hard work in the first 10 years; then lots of fun in the next 20!

> There is a price for success, and it is always paid in advance.

I encourage everyone to create a new sense of urgency. It doesn't have to be the beginning of a new year for you to create a sense of urgency. Capture the moment of the calendar year we are in. As Leo Tolstoy said in *What Men Live by and Other Tales*, "There is only one time that is important — Now! It is the most important time because it is the only time we have power over." And Dr. Napoleon Hill, who wrote the 1937 best seller *Think and Grow Rich*, said, "Most misfortunes are the result of misused time." I would like to take the liberty of revising that just a bit to say instead that "most *missed fortunes* are the results of misused time."

Embrace Hard Work

The longer I stayed in this business, and the more I learned about being successful, the more I came to appreciate a truth that has been around for all time: Hard work is the key to success. It's not technology or a fancy presentation; it's about getting out and seeing people.

A long time ago, I was told that some LIMRA researchers cold-called businesses and homes in the Hartford, Connecticut, area. They knocked on a substantial number of doors. They were told to ask only one very simple question: "You wouldn't want to buy any life insurance today, would you?" To their amazement, even using this less-than-desirable approach, one in 53 people said yes. My guess is that that result would be similar today.

The point is that if you made enough calls, even using poorly phrased questions, you could probably find enough people to keep you in business. This might not sound desirable to you, but it does prove the point that if failure is not an option, there is a way.

Any top producer will tell you that making hard work a habit will lead to a happier and more rewarding life. As I have said, "Good habits are hard to form but easy to live with; bad habits are easy to form but hard to live with."

I came across the Mental Equipment Checklist from the famous Dr. Napoleon Hill, one of the early authors of personal-success literature, and I would like to share it with you.[17] The fifth quality Dr. Hill lists is hard work.

It is a list of desirable qualities that almost any normal and reasonable person can adopt and apply. The list is long, and perfection may be attained only slowly. Therefore, before entering into a detailed consideration of the things you would like your mind and body to be capable of doing, let's first enumerate those that are absolutely necessary.

- **Physical fitness** *is of tremendous importance for the simple reason that neither mind nor body can function well without it. Therefore, give attention to your habits of life, proper diet, healthful exercise, and fresh air.*

- **Courage** *must be a part of every man or woman who succeeds in any undertaking, especially that of selling in these trying times of intense competition after a devastating period of depression and discouragement.*

- **Imagination** *is an absolute requisite of a successful salesman. He must anticipate situations and even objections on the part of his prospective customer. He must have such a lively imagination as to enable its operation to place him in sympathetic understanding with the position, needs, and objectives of his customer. He must almost literally stand in the other man's shoes. This takes real imagination.*

- **Speech**. *The tone of voice must be pleasing. A high-pitched, squeaky voice is irritating. Words half-swallowed are hard to understand. Speak distinctly and enunciate clearly. A meek voice indicates a weak person. A firm, clean-cut, clear voice that moves with assurance and color indicates an aggressive person with enthusiasm and aggressiveness.*

- **Hard work** *is the only thing that will turn sales training and ability into money. No amount of good health, courage, or imagination is worth a dime unless it is put to work, and the amount of pay a salesman gets is usually fixed by the amount of very hard, intelligent work that he actually puts out. Many people sidestep this factor of success.*[18]

---

[17] Napoleon Hill. *How to Sell Your Way Through Life*, 1955, Ralston Publishing Co., Cleveland, Ohio, pps. 72-73.
[18] Ibid (emphasis added).

Find Inspiration from Within

One thing I have learned after 40-plus years of leading people is that while I can *motivate* people, only an individual can *inspire* himself or herself. Motivation is external, whereas inspiration is an inside job. We attempt to motivate people to do things that we know are ultimately good for them. We motivate people to reach new levels of productivity and income. We motivate people to get out of their comfort zone and grow. And growth is often painful.

But inspiration comes from within. *To be inspired, people have to know how the activities they engage in are connected directly to their core values.* That is where an organization's mission comes from. When we looked at the top 10 percent of our reps, we found a group who ranked in the top 2 percent of all producers in the industry. What an accomplishment! These individuals were never flash-in-the-pan producers — no one big case does it. Instead, they fit a profile of what all consistent top producers do. They build a long-term clientele while helping people get what they want out of life. They truly believe that every life matters, that every life is worth insuring.

What differentiates top producers? First of all, they take advantage of both *external motivation* and *internal inspiration*. These are the people who qualify for every contest because they know it is an opportunity for growth. Whether it's a trip to Puerto Rico or a dinner at Morton's, they are always there. Being a winner is important to them. Forum reps are driven by lifestyle — I don't mean fancy cars, but rather the elements that really make a difference, such as the neighborhood or community they live in, the schools their children attend, and the trips they take that broaden their children's outlook and experience.

Ultimately, top producers begin to think about their legacy. They also think about the impact they have every day on the people they serve.

Have Integrity, Intelligence, and Energy

As I will discuss in more detail in Chapter 9, only 20 percent of the people on the planet have the ability to sell anything. Those who have that talent should use it to improve the lives of others and their own lives.

One manager I know said he would ask a low activity producer why he or she was choosing to be selfish. His point was that we should be offering more people our help in these challenging times (and offering a better living to our families). Why see seven to 10 people each week when we could be seeing 12 to 15 — or more? This is not about a work ethic or lack of one (and suggesting so never works anyway) because we are all basically lazy. But questioning someone's integrity will fire up a person who has integrity.

Mega-investor and business magnate Warren Buffett said, "In looking for people to hire, you look for three qualities: integrity, intelligence, and energy. And if they don't have the first, then the last two will kill you."

On the subject of integrity, I offer a different view — that integrity can sometimes be a road block to commitment. I know this sounds strange, but I believe it is true. People of integrity can get into a conflict with their own laziness. In other words, they hesitate to make a commitment because they know that if they do so, their integrity will make them keep it.

In contrast, people with little integrity tend to throw commitments around because they never really mean to keep them in the first place. They just like the way it sounds. So people of integrity need to set up their environment to help them overcome their laziness and put their integrity to work.

Once we have the integrity part of the equation figured out, we can use intelligence to learn our task and our energy to perform it. But without integrity, we have people who think they can use their intelligence to outsmart us and their energy to evade us. People who lack integrity will be the death of you. Over the years, we have become pretty good at finding people who are in that 20 percent category of those who can sell, but finding people with high integrity levels to match is more difficult to discover in the time period we have in the selection process.

Handle Adversity Well

Several years ago while speaking in Singapore, I had the opportunity to meet Dr. Paul G. Stoltz.[19] Paul is now a friend, and he and I have talked often about the direct relationship between a person's ability to deal with adversity and his or her success in our business. In my opinion, resilience — your capacity to thrive in adversity — is as important as, and marries perfectly with, trust. I'll explain.

Dr. Stoltz is the world's leading expert on measuring and strengthening human resilience and works with top companies and top performers worldwide. He has developed a profile that people can take to assess their Adversity Quotient®, or AQ.® The AQ Profile® can be completed in eight to 10 minutes and provides a wealth of insight about an individual. Harvard Business School uses this tool in its Executive Education programs.[20]

[19] http://adversityadvantage.com/stoltz.html

[20] According to Harvard Business School, AQ is the most widely adopted assessment in the world for gauging one's Adversity Quotient, or resilience. The AQ profile is available at www.hoopis.com.

In 2010, Dr. Stoltz agreed to allow the first 150 people who responded to my Forum Focus blog post to take his AQ Profile free of charge. Once the reps completed the profile, they received their AQ scores, and Dr. Stoltz shared with them methods for increasing their AQ. It had a tremendous impact on the reps.

AQ is about how you respond to life, especially the tough stuff. It is a measure of how you respond to and deal with everything, from everyday hassles to the big adversities that life can spring on you. It is also an established science, theory, and approach for becoming measurably more resilient. The more resilient you are, the more effectively and constructively you respond to life's difficulties, and the more fulfilling life becomes.

Even without knowing your AQ score, you can begin to improve. Here's the rule of thumb: The stronger your AQ, the more effectively you will respond to adversity and the less life's events will take a toll on your energy, performance, health, and outlook. The weaker your AQ, the more difficult it can be for you to maintain the energy, optimism, and fortitude required to optimize your talents and, by extension, your life.

When the markets collapsed a few years ago, trust in the financial services industry imploded. From Bernie Madoff to Merrill Lynch, trust in the industry and its professionals plunged to an all-time low. So demonstrating authentic trustworthiness emerged as a true competitive advantage. But maybe in these adversity-rich times, trust is no longer enough to earn clients' dollars.

There are plenty of academic definitions of trust, but few compare to the common-sense litmus test: Would you let that person babysit your kids? When we hand over our assets and place them under the management of an advisor, this is essentially what we're doing. We are saying, "I trust you to take brilliant care of the accumulated rewards from my blood, sweat, tears, and years." We trust people based on their competence — their acumen for figuring out the best moves — and their character — the moral foundation to do the right thing. If the competence and character are strong, then we should trust the advisor with our "children," right? Not necessarily.

Trust is meaningless until tested by adversity. Think about it. Which do you care about more: how an advisor behaves when everything is great, or how he or she behaves when everything goes wrong? Which reveals the advisor's true competence and character? It is in the flames of adversity that one's character is both revealed and forged. Unfortunately, the industry faltered and fell, rather than rallying and shining in the face of real adversity.

The only genuine path to authentic trust is, therefore, through exceptional *resilience*. Being your best in the most adverse moments, shining your brightest lights in the darkest days is how you forge that unique brand of deep, impenetrable, enduring trust.

One thing is clear: Being able to deal with adversity is a key ingredient to success. Adversity is a part of our daily lives. The more we allow it to distract and disturb us, the more difficult it becomes to focus on the things we need to do to become successful.

> Being your best in the most adverse moments, shining your brightest lights in the darkest days is how you forge that unique brand of deep, impenetrable, enduring trust.

Persevere: Drill through the Wall

Let's say there is a wall separating you from everything you want in life. If you can just drill through that wall, it's all yours, all the good stuff, the things you want most in life for you and your family. I can hand you the drill and tell you to get started, but what I cannot tell you is how thick the wall is. There is no way to know its thickness; you just have to keep drilling, without giving up. Do you have the stamina and determination to do it?

These are the circumstances we face every day. You know that what you want is behind the wall, but you give up. Your arms become heavy and tired. You settle for what's left outside the wall, even though it's not what you want. Remember, Albert Gray said, "It's easier to adjust to the hardship of making a poor living than it is to adjust to the hardship of making a better one."

I believe it's our job as leaders to give you the drill — the tool — which is the training and development and the right environment. The rest is up to you. You must do the work, even though you're uncertain about how thick the wall is or how long it will take you to reach your goal. And to make the job easier, there are diamond drill bits — new clients available for your use — included for *free*! Every new client makes it easier to drill through that wall.

Years ago, a rep came into my office and told me he had just had a bad night. After asking why, he told me that he had to tell his kids he was cancelling their planned trip to Disney World because he did not make his goals for the year. I replied, "Don't ever let your children pay the price for your lack of self-discipline." That has become a rule of life for me; why not you, too?

Here's what professional golfer Jack Nicklaus once said about one of his opponents who didn't make it on the tour: "He had a lot of talent, but didn't have much dedication, wasn't organized, didn't know how to comprehend what he was doing, didn't try to learn how to get better." That's a pretty powerful appraisal of not getting it done. I cannot begin to tell you how many great people came through my door, went through my training program, and just could not make it work. Just like Jack Nicklaus said!

If you follow these guidelines, you will be on your way to becoming a top producer who excels and thrives in this business and gains the trust of more clients than you ever thought possible.

And believe me, behind the wall is everything you want. Behind the wall lies the Bountiful Life.

Eleven Characteristics, Traits, and Methods of Top Sales Reps

In the last chapter, I identified the habits and strategies of top producers and suggested that if you are not among the top producers, you can join that elite group by studying what they do and then emulating them.

These are the 11 characteristics, traits, and methods of top sales reps:

"Courage is the first of human qualities because it is the quality which guarantees the others."

—Aristotle

1. The five Cs of success (confidence, courage, competitiveness, commitment, and communication)

2. Leverage of size

3. A focus on relationships

4. An emphasis on marketing

5. Specialization or creation of a niche

6. Professional referral networks

7. Nonprofit organization involvement

8. The team

9. An emphasis on wealth management

10. Commitment to service

11. Time management

I have been fortunate to be a member of the Research Agencies Group (RAG) for more than 30 years. The RAG study group was created in 1931 under the auspices of LIMRA International. It is composed of 20 agency leaders from different companies. Every two or three years, each member is responsible for conducting research on a specific topic and presenting the findings at one of the RAG meetings, which are held each May and November. It's a great group of people.

In May 2011, one of our members, John Kerr, presented a paper entitled "Characteristics, Traits, and Methods of Top Advisors." John conducted research that included numerous interviews and surveys to determine what top advisors do that is different from what average producers do — in other words, what leads to top advisors' exceptional production. The results gave leaders and advisors a lot to think about as they look for ways to increase productivity. John's research uncovered the 11 characteristics I present in this chapter. Implementing any one of them could lead to greater success. Use this chapter as a personal development program for your business.

My colleague's study revealed the characteristics of average producers as well as top producers. It is important to look at the average producers' traits to see how they compare with the top producers' traits.

In this study, producers were asked questions such as:

- What do you do best?

- What do you believe has accounted for your success?

- How do you see yourself as different from other advisors?

- How did you start prospecting? How has it evolved?

- How do you service your clients?

- Why do you think people do business with you?

- Do you have a specialization?

- How is your team structured?

- How do you spend your time?

- Where do you find new prospects?

These are great questions, and I recommend that you stop right now and answer these questions in writing so that you can compare your answers to those of the top advisors.

Here are answers given by *average* producers:

- "I'm chasing the business, not running it."

- "It's a people-driven practice. It's totally dependent on me."

- "Lack of operational controls and consistency; everything is done a little different each time."

- "Difficulty with focus and execution; great ideas, but unable to execute on them in a way that moves the needle."

- "Revenue doesn't reflect opportunity. I should be more profitable than I am. I've been doing this for 10 or 15 years, but ..."

- "Not creating business value. This business could be the largest potential asset one has."

- "Business consumes life."

Top advisors gave very different answers because they had overcome most, if not all, of these issues because they embody the 11 characteristics and use the best methods of top-performing advisors.

One: The Five C's of Success

Top advisors share a common mindset toward this business. That mindset drives and forms the foundation of everything they do and is characterized by five words that begin with the letter C.

- **Confidence**. Developed over time, the goal is to get prospects to believe in you so they will listen to your advice and follow your recommendations. Top advisors have confidence in the tremendous value proposition they have for the people they work with. They are passionate and enthusiastic about this and feel they do the best job possible. As you think about your value proposition, ask yourself whether you are passionate and enthusiastic about it. *What would it take for you to get more excited about what you do for your clients?*

- **Courage**. Top advisors are willing to take risks and move out of their comfort zone. This applies to marketing, overcoming rejection, and implementing ideas. One advisor likes to say he has a high "IQ" — *implementation* quotient. If he has a good idea, or hears one, he will follow his instincts and make it happen. This is a common trait among top producers. As Albert Gray said, "Successful people make habits of doing things unsuccessful people don't like to do." *What ideas have you implemented recently?*

- **Competitiveness**. Top advisors are goal-oriented. One consultant who was interviewed said that every one of the advisors he worked with could tell him what their goals were and where they stood in terms of reaching them. In short, top advisors keep score. *Are your goals in writing? Are you keeping score?*

- **Commitment.** Top advisors have a tremendous work ethic. Almost all of them said it was the extraordinary work they did early in their careers that distinguished them from their peers and contributed to their success. The top advisors continue working about 50 hours a week, although the definition of work has changed to emphasize the right activities, such as spending more time with clients and prospects. Again, easy jobs don't pay much. There is a price for success, and it is always paid in advance. *How strong is your work ethic?*

- **Communication.** Top advisors are effective communicators, especially one-on-one. They can relate to their market niche, project confidence, and engender trust. They are excellent listeners, and while one-half claim to have developed world-class presentations, they acknowledge that presentation skills are not as critical as one-on-one communication skills are. *How are your communication skills? How do you build trust?*

Two: Leverage of Size

Leverage of size is about working intentionally in a high-net-worth market.

The study from RAG mentions the John Todd Formula. John Todd was a company and industry legend and was the founding general agent of the Hoopis Agency in 1943. John was the quintessential top producer, and he built an organization in Evanston, Illinois, that provided service to thousands of clients. His formula for success was as follows:

Production = Average Case Size x Number of Cases x Closing Ratio

The closing ratio can obviously not exceed 100 percent, but, theoretically, average case size and number of cases can expand infinitely. Top producers look at this formula and focus on case size. The top producers know that by focusing on case size, they *prospect* differently, *learn* differently, and *think* differently.

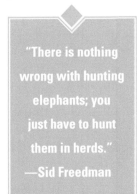

"There is nothing wrong with hunting elephants; you just have to hunt them in herds."

—Sid Freedman

The great Sid Freedman, who was one of this country's most sought-after speakers on financial planning, personal motivation, career development, and time management, said, "There is nothing wrong with hunting elephants; you just have to hunt them in herds." Top advisors learn how to hunt clients in herds.

For those who aspire to that type of activity, here is what you have to do.

First, using John Todd's formula, focus on your *closing ratio.* You need to improve this skill as much as possible. What's more, it's a bit of a lost art. Many people who are good closers do it very naturally. In *Trustworthy Selling,* this is called "gaining commitment." There are many things you can do to improve your closing ratio, and until you achieve the near impossible 100 percent closing ratio, you need to work on improving this skill.

The second piece of the formula is the *number of cases.* The key to a long, sustainable, successful career is high lives. Very few top producers make it big without high-lives activity. This is particularly true in the early years of a person's career. You need to make the changes necessary to get your lives above 100 and growing.

The third piece of the John Todd Formula is *average case size.* The best way to increase this is gradually. John Todd said many times that a rep should specialize for about one year before leaving the business. John's organization, which worked with many Fortune 500 companies, employed a broad approach. I remember John coming into my office to tell me he was working on a great case. My thought was that he was referring to millions of premium coming in, but then he went on to describe a case he opened on his barber.

So begin by trying to open one to two additional cases per month, and do it through joint work. Incorporate one question into your prospecting language: "Who do you know who might benefit from meeting one of our estate planning or business insurance experts?" You can add any number of specialists to this question, but it presents a different picture to your nominator. Consumers are used to the idea of specialization. Try it. Doctors and lawyers do it because it's necessary, given the complexities of their work. Insist that your joint-work specialist be willing to teach you along the way; it's probably how he or she learned the specialization, too.

If you commit to finding two new joint-work cases per month, you will open 24 additional cases per year. This should result in six to eight more cases being closed in a year. The better large cases have an average premium of $20,000 to $30,000. This means your share of the joint work should be approximately $100,000 in premium. If you add $100,000 of premium on top of 100 lives, at an average case size for a newer rep of $1,500 of premium, you will have $250,000 of premium.

Yes, it's as easy as that. Do the heavy lifting. Build the base. Open two additional joint-work cases per month, and let the expert put the icing on your cake. Specialists should also be reaching out to new reps and telling them what they are looking for in an ideal prospect. In my former agency,

30 percent of our agency business was done through joint work. One plus one equals three!

So review your prospecting techniques and start working on average case size as a goal.

Three: A Focus on Relationships

The third characteristic that top sales reps share is a focus on relationships. Top advisors spend the majority of their time on the relationship part of the business. Most report spending 75 percent of their time on relationships and only 25 percent of their time on reading, research, administration, proposal preparation, learning, and so on. I remember Joe Gandolfo, a super producer from years ago, saying this business is 2 percent product knowledge and 98 percent people skills. While things might be a little different today, the people skills are still the most important in building relationships.

> Top producers keep good notes and watch for opportunities to spend time with their top clients in environments they both enjoy.

A study conducted by MDRT a few years ago showed the importance of time spent in front of prospects and clients. The study revealed that a base member of MDRT spent 19 percent of his or her time in front of prospects and clients. Court of the Table members, who produce at three times base, spent 48 percent of their time with prospects and clients. And Top of the Table members, who produce at six times base, spent 53 percent of their time with prospects and clients.

Remarkably, these top performers also had fine-tuned their businesses and reported working only 52 hours per week, while the base member worked 59 hours per week. Imagine that: having six times the production while working almost 30 fewer hours per month. That's a lot of extra family time. So spending time with clients and prospects is well worth it. Remember, part of the Bountiful Life includes having the time and money to do more for your family, religious organization, and community.

Top producers set up systems to ensure that they spend more time with clients. Their systems include, but are not limited to, activities like golf, golf clinics, sporting events, dinners, wine tastings, hunting trips, and theater events. Top advisors know all about their clients, including their likes and dislikes. They keep good notes and watch for opportunities to spend time with their top clients in environments they both enjoy. Top producers invest a lot in these activities. Because it's too important to leave it to chance.

How do you focus on your clients? What is your plan? What is your budget?

One advisor in the RAG survey made this comment: "Most of the products and services we provide have no guaranteed outcome and are completely intangible. Yet because of their relative importance, financial advisors are often chosen on a gut instinct that is connected to a high level of trust. In fact, what financial advisors are really selling is trust."

Spending time with clients is a great way to demonstrate the four characteristics of trust: benevolence, integrity, dependability, and competency. These characteristics answer the questions: Do I care? Can you trust me? Will I follow through? Do I know what I am talking about? The more time you spend with your clients, the more they will learn how well these traits characterize you.

Create a plan to spend more time in front of clients and prospects. Start by tracking the amount of time you currently spend with them. Remember, measurement improves performance. Don't just estimate, calculate. Figure out how much money you can spend in this area and find thoughtful ways to do so. You don't need to be extravagant, just thoughtful. The key is to show your interest in your clients and their families.

Four: An Emphasis on Marketing

There are many ways for a rep to incorporate marketing into their business. However, there are three primary reasons most advisors don't do event marketing. The first is that they don't know how to do it effectively. Second, they are not willing to face the inevitable rejection that comes with marketing. And third, they are not willing to invest in marketing.

The top advisors in the MDRT study used many marketing strategies such as:

- Obtaining client referrals

- Marketing to professional networks

- Niche marketing

- Event marketing

- Right-place, right-people marketing

  Let's review each.

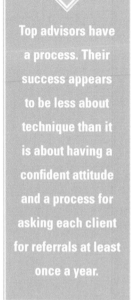

Top advisors have a process. Their success appears to be less about technique than it is about having a confident attitude and a process for asking each client for referrals at least once a year.

Client Referrals

Obtaining client referrals is the first marketing strategy. You may not think of referrals as a marketing strategy, but it is. Everyone knows the importance of getting referrals, yet the average advisor does not have a real plan for doing it.

We know from LIMRA Research that 78 percent of clients prefer to be referred to a trusted advisor and that 90 percent said they would provide a referral to an advisor who has done a good job for them. In *Cultivating the Middle-Class Millionaire: Why Financial Advisors Are Failing Their Wealthy Clients and What They Can Do About It* by David A. Geracioti and Russ Alan Prince, 70 percent of the most satisfied clients said they were likely to refer their advisors, but fewer than 11 percent were asked.

Top advisors have a process. Their success appears to be less about technique than it is about having a confident attitude and a process for asking each client for referrals at least once a year. Top advisors always mention the need to focus on A+ clients and to let their clients know they want referrals.

Network, Niche, and Event Marketing

Nearly all top advisors use event marketing to reward loyal clients or their professional referral network while at the same time using it as an opportunity to uncover new prospects. Many advisors work through other professionals such as lawyers and CPAs to hold targeted events for their best clients.

To spend time with their clients, top advisors hold unique events rather than more traditional product-type ones. One example is an event one advisor held for female clients called "Anti-Aging: How to Live Longer, Maintain Energy, and Manage Life's Stress." The advisor asked a nutritionist, a trainer, a dermatologist, and a psychologist to participate. Each was given 20 minutes to speak, and each had a table set up with information to give out.

The advisor invited his best female clients and extended the invitation to the clients' bridge clubs, book clubs, and other friends, knowing their circles would include other accomplished women. At the end of the presentation, he did a short commercial explaining how he works with clients to reduce financial stress. He concluded by offering a future meeting.

In addition to rewarding clients or referral sources, the key behind this marketing technique is getting clients to help the advisor. The events provide an easy, nonthreatening venue that a client can invite other potential clients to. *The bottom line: Top advisors have a specific strategy in place for event marketing.*

Right Place, Right People

The fifth marketing strategy, right-place, right-people, is about the ability to put yourself in a position to meet affluent individuals, build relationships, and over time transition many of these relationships into business. The art of converting these relationships to business is key.

Many advisors in the study felt it just happened — as opposed to it being a strategy and technique. It seems to happen "naturally" to people who are involved in their community or in niche markets. Having good relationship building skills was the most important item cited.

As the story is told, when the infamous bank robber Willie Sutton was asked why he robbed banks, his answer was simple but profound: "Because that's where the money is." This clarity of focus provides a useful lesson. As you think about right-place, right-people marketing, ask yourself where the money is. Country club memberships for advisors who enjoy golf should be mandatory. And now is a great time to join a club, because the economy has left many clubs wanting for new members.

There are many ways to meet good people, but it requires a plan. Rarely does it happen by accident. You should never join a club solely to do business, but instead should do so to meet people of similar interests and to give them a chance to see you at your very best as a trustworthy selling professional.

Five: Specialization or Development of a Niche

Specialization or development of a niche is a natural step for a top advisor. Niche marketing occurs within a specialization. Affluent clients ask, "Why should I do business with you?" Top advisors are able to answer, "Because I specialize in working with individuals like you." Defining your ideal client is an important step in this process. *Matching your talents, interests, and education to this clientele is key*. You cannot have a specialization if you don't define one.

When I think of niche marketing, I think more about the people than the specialization. You can specialize in a certain subject area, such as estate planning, business insurance, BOLI/COLI (bank-owned life insurance/corporate-owned life insurance), or retirement planning. Or you can specialize in working with a group of people like accountants, lawyers,

CEOs, small business owners, pharmacists, or professors. In either case, you must develop special knowledge, skills, and understanding to work in a specialization or niche.

Remember what John Todd said: "An agent should specialize about one year before he or she wants to go out of the business." I have always suggested that the move to a specialization or a niche should be made slowly so you don't put all your eggs in one basket.

Be aware of the kind of people you relate to best. Getting referrals from one to another is the easiest way to make a move into a niche. If it's accountants who you like to work with, learn all you can about their association benefits. Understand the issues they face in their businesses. When you speak with accountants, know the obstacles and opportunities they deal with every day and be able to articulate and speak intelligently about them. Specialists create a barrier to entry for other advisors by putting themselves in a position to provide more value to clients than less-focused and less-knowledgeable advisors can.

Ultimately, your goal is to create a sense among your clients that because of special training, knowledge, and approaches, you are a trusted advisor.

Earlier, we learned that the four factors of trust are benevolence, integrity, dependability, and competency, with competency as the least important of the four factors, because we are considered competent until we prove otherwise. Specialists or niche marketers focus on dependability and competency to make their mark. It defines who they are.

Several advisors have suggested that their goal is to become "*a* trusted advisor," not "*the* trusted advisor." Those who follow this approach look to become part of a team. They build relationships with CPA firms that look to them to provide specific knowledge in the area of risk management.

The bottom line in the specialization and niche-marketing plan is to define your market, know your client, and know your stuff. Doing that comes back to immersing yourself in lifelong learning. Participating in online training, home office schools, and industry meetings, while also spending time with others who work in your desired space, are all mandatory steps in this process. The way to learn is by subjecting yourself to training. Listen to speakers who sound over your head. Listen over and over. Over time, the message will get through. Listening over and over and not being afraid to ask questions is the best way to learn your niche.

So define your ideal clientele and then prospect toward it. It will not happen by chance; it must be done by choice. The top advisors are always looking for people in their marketplace, and they know how to ask the questions that will get them there. This is called your "defining identity."

Knowing the who, what, and why of your niche is the most important step in becoming a trustworthy selling professional.

Six: Professional Referral Networks

Professional referral networks are one of the key marketing functions of top advisors. As I mentioned earlier, 78 percent of people would like to be referred to a trusted advisor; 90 percent of clients say they are willing to give referrals, yet only 11 percent say they are asked. The No. 1 referral to a trusted advisor comes from professionals like CPAs. *What are you doing to cultivate these valuable relationships?*

> The No. 1 way millionaires find their advisors is through a referral from a trusted professional.

In *The Millionaire Next Door*, Thomas Stanley tells us that the No. 1 way millionaires find their advisors is through a referral from a trusted professional. However, when Russell Prince surveyed financial advisors, he found that professional referrals account for only 30 percent of their new clients, while client referrals accounted for the majority. Stephanie Bogan is an industry speaker, writer, and expert on practice management.[21] Her survey of more than 400 financial advisors found that the top quartile of advisors found referrals from other professionals 21 percent more effective than reported by the other three quartiles. There seems to be a disconnect between how millionaires choose their advisors and how most advisors acquire their millionaire clients. The very top advisors report that a much higher percentage of their new clients come from other professionals.

So while we seem to understand the importance of getting referrals from other trusted professionals, we don't seem to ask as much as we should. People are far more willing to give referrals than we acknowledge. Most advisors don't ask out of fear of facing rejection. The best way to overcome this reluctance is to read the research on the willingness of people to refer.

Great research left on a shelf is just taking up valuable space. On the other hand, great research turned into facts and language to use with a prospect or client is priceless. When I know that one in six people have a plan for retirement, and I mention this to a prospect or client, they immediately begin to think about people they know and care about and realize they need a plan. That is how you turn a fact into a prospecting technique.

---

[21] http://www.financial-planning.com/advisormax/coaches/bogan.html

Within days of our first *Trustworthy Selling* training session, young reps found that this fact could get them referred to older people. A pretty good use of research, wouldn't you agree?

Whether it is a friend or relative, a client, a professional advisor, or someone else, the fact is people want referrals to trusted advisors. So you need to ask. *You have to ask.* But first you need to earn the right to ask. You need to cultivate relationships with other professionals so they will think of you when they need insurance and investment advice. Top advisors know that building a professional referral network is essential to their success. There are many ways to do this, but one that many use is joining the associations of other professionals as associate members. Often this is allowed as a way to bring in outside services and revenue. Showing up at their meetings is a great way to become known. Joining clubs is another way to meet these professionals.

Of course, some of the traditional methods also work well, such as golf events, client-appreciation events, and special learning opportunities that can enhance your image with clients.

Seven: Nonprofit Organization Involvement

Involvement in nonprofit organizations is so important to top advisors that it is a subject unto itself. When listening to the introductions of top corporate leaders, have you ever heard one that didn't include the mention of several organizations they were involved with? Like me, you probably think, "Where do they find the time to do all that stuff?" Well, as the saying goes, "If you have an important job to get done, give it to the busiest person." I believe it is true that busy people get more done because they are better organized, and they thrive on accomplishment.

There are many types of organizations, and it doesn't seem to matter much which ones you choose. It's just important to get involved. Organizations focus on every imaginable cause: a symphony, a critical illness, a poverty-related issue, an alumni association, a social issue. The list is seemingly endless.

Whichever organizations you choose, you will always find two things that are important to them: fundraising and membership — two great activities for people like us to get involved in. Whether you are selling a financial product, making a donation, or telling others about the importance of membership, they are all things a good salesperson in any field can do. They are also the positions non-sales types dislike, so there's a real advantage because we know that those are the two most important functions of any organization, and we're good at them. In fact, if you join and then volunteer for one of those jobs, they will look at you like you are crazy. But that's OK.

Top advisors know that by joining these organizations, they can showcase their talents and expertise for the nonprofits while at the same time meeting many of the most prominent and influential members of the community. Being a leader in these organizations gives them exposure to highly affluent prospects and the opportunity to build relationships around mutual interests. Having mutual interests is critical.

Never join an organization to do business. Join because it's the right thing to do in your desire to give back to society. Choose something you are passionate about. Perhaps a family member has been affected by a disease or you want to support a cause. Maybe you wouldn't have the opportunities you have today if it were not for an organization or person you met. The more passionate you are about the organizations and causes you support, the more others will respect you for your enthusiasm and will want to know you. It's the circle of success that can impact so many aspects of our lives.

> The more passionate you are about the organizations and causes you support, the more others will respect you for your enthusiasm and will want to know you.

Being involved in nonprofit organizations is a good thing. It demonstrates both benevolence and integrity, two key factors of trust. Being an active member of these organizations also demonstrates competence and dependability. Now you are embodying all four factors of trust.

Eight: The Team

The team is an incredibly important part of top advisors' success. It is nearly impossible to succeed at a high level without good people. It's been said that people never succeed alone; they only fail alone. Truer words have never been spoken, especially when we look at the work of top advisors.

I have seen too many reps either fail or stunt their growth by failing to understand this important fact. Advisors need to build a business. *This is no longer a job for just a salesperson. This is a career for a businessperson who also happens to be in sales.* I have always believed that nothing happens until something is sold. So every business needs a salesperson.

Top advisors build a vertical team to support them. This structure enables the top advisor to do what he or she does best: build and develop client and prospect relationships and bring in new business. Advisors generally start with a single staff person and then grow as needed. Smart advisors hire before they think they need new staff, because if they are to continue to grow, they want to do so without losing valuable momentum.

Top advisors want to sell, not manage. So try to hire self-starters, people who are capable of managing themselves. I once had a top rep whose sole staff person suggested she needed more help to handle all the business the advisor was generating. The advisor wisely suggested that she hire an assistant. This made the staff person feel important and, more importantly, shifted the management duties to her as well. Brilliant! I have suggested this to many reps since then. That team today consists of two top advisors, two junior associates, and five staff people. What a great example of team building.

The top advisors from the RAG study said that, as their businesses grew, they realized they needed to attract and retain the best people to support them. Many of them noted that their teams changed over the years, but virtually everyone remarked about the quality and competency of their current staff.

They appear to be very generous to their staff, often compensating them at a significantly higher level than what they could earn with another employer. They felt this was warranted because turnover costs much more than generous compensation. There are many ways to compensate good staff, but one strategy that was common was giving out bonuses tied to the advisor's production and success.

Steve Sanduski, CFP, whose company, Peak Advisor Alliance, offers consulting to more than 1,000 advisors, suggests rating each staff person as A+, A, B, C, or D.[22] The descriptions of each category are:

- **"A+" staff members are the ones you want to clone.** A+ staff have great personalities and outstanding work habits. They show initiative and get the job done, no matter what it takes.

- **"A" staff are your bread-and-butter employees.** They're not quite as good as A+, but they are definitely keepers and can help you get where you want to go. With a little more training and direction, they may be able to move up to A+.

- **"B" employees are good people but just don't exert the extra oomph needed, or their job might not be designed to take full advantage of their talents and interests.** To provide these employees with needed direction, Steve suggests establishing a 90-day plan

[22] http://www.peakadvisoralliance.com

with proper training and possibly shifting some responsibilities to other employees.

- **"C" employees are similar to B staffers, except it is clear they are never going to move up a level.**

- **"D" employees shouldn't be on the payroll.**

Steve says the hard part is that the C and D employees have to go. B staff members are on the bubble. Give them 90 days of direction and training and work with them, and if they can move up a level, great. If not, they must go also. Anecdotal evidence from top advisors shows that they have a very high percentage of A+ and A staff members, and they are very proud of them.

One position that showed up repeatedly was a person hired to help advisors with marketing. These staff people have solid relationships in the advisor's niche market and can provide access to it. Others, particularly investment advisors, hire public relations firms to help increase the advisor's prominence and number of speaking engagements through various media opportunities, including print and television.

The one thing we all agree on is that it is hard to achieve at a high level without a high-level staff. Advisors need to focus on hiring staff as soon as possible. As the great management consultant Peter Drucker said, always have the lowest paid person capable of doing the task do the task. This means that you, as the rainmaker, cannot be tied down with tasks that are best delegated to another person who probably will do them better than you would. *When you find highly competent staff members, pay them well, reward them, and above all, treat them right.*

Nine: An Emphasis on Wealth Management

A significant percentage of top advisors define their business as a wealth-management practice as opposed to that of a financial planner or an investment advisor. Wealth management is defined as "the comprehensive and holistic process that integrates the long-term goals of an individual with financial solutions using a planning-based approach."

The RAG study found that the only major exception to the wealth-management approach was with top life insurance producers. The very top people in the field generally do not aspire to offer comprehensive services, but instead focus on a niche requiring life insurance as part of a solution. This ranges from the so-called insurance geek to the COLI/BOLI specialist to the expert in premium financing to the subpar specialist whose mantra is, "Bring old, wealthy, and sick clients."

There are many options for today's reps. Generally speaking, your choices will be determined by your prospects and your education. As always, the important thing for a rep who is interested in building the business is to find time to study. The balancing act is key. While working to see people and provide service, you still have to find time to sharpen your saw. Lifelong learning is key to your success.

We know from The American College that income rises as you acquire designations. CLUs make more than those without that designation; ChFCs make more than a rep who has only a CLU, and so forth. *Knowledge is power, and it helps reps overcome call reluctance.*

In the Stephanie Bogan survey mentioned earlier, she found that reps who focus on wealth management earn 220 percent more than those who identify themselves as financial planners and 147 percent more than investment managers. This, of course, can be a function of relative age and affluence of their clients.

The bottom line: If you prospect where the money is and you educate yourself to serve that market, you will have a great career. You can't be in this business as a career and not pursue the professional designations of the career. Think about it. Would you choose a bookkeeper over a CPA? You make a choice every day about what your future will look like in this business. *Make the right choices!*

Ten: A Commitment to Service

Raving fans are loyal, affluent clients who provide more referrals, bring in more assets, and do more business than clients who are simply satisfied.

One elite advisor in the RAG survey said that the investment management business has, to a great degree, become a commodity. He differentiates himself by providing "world-class service." Management consultant and author Ken Blanchard wrote, "Raving fan clients are instrumental to success."

Raving fans are loyal, affluent clients who provide more referrals, bring in more assets, and do more business than clients who are simply satisfied.

When asked about service, Bogan said, "The biggest difference in the service of top advisors as compared to others is being proactive and high-touch." These differences give the client the sense that the advisor and the advisor's team are in control of matters and have time to provide exceptional service. All client surveys indicate that the reason most clients leave an advisor is that they don't hear from him or her often enough.

We have seen this repeatedly in our industry since the difficult years that began around 2008. When the market first collapsed, we didn't know what to expect. Our advice to reps was simply to keep in touch with clients, let them know you care, and reassure them that you are monitoring market conditions. We quickly learned this is just what they needed, someone to talk to. When we look back over the last few years, we know two things for certain: First, we didn't lose clients, and second, we gained even more — through referrals from current clients. In other words, the phone calls, the attention to detail, and the high-touch service all paid off with the result of satisfied clients.

Contact your A+ and A clients at least 12 to 18 times each year. These contacts should be planned and varied. Top advisors in the RAG survey shared a list of strategies for working with these important clients:

- Send welcome letters to new clients.

- Provide a terrific client experience, particularly in the first 90 days.

- Reach out to new clients to make sure they understand the reporting and have no further questions.

- Perform random acts of kindness.

- Provide prompt and accurate responses to questions.

- Have a person in the office when a client calls.

- Send invitations to events that clients would enjoy.

- Send birthday and anniversary cards.

- Hold well-prepared, comprehensive review meetings.

- Ensure systematic "touches" by the advisor or staff.

Use these strategies to start every client off with a great experience and to build a clientele of loyal, raving fans.

Eleven: Time Management

It's certainly no surprise that time management is on the list of top advisors' methods. Remember the paradox of time? No one has enough, but we all have all there is. Each of us is given the same 24 hours a day, seven days per week, for a total of 168 hours each week. No one gets a minute more or a minute less, and it really is up to you to choose how to use your time that makes all the difference in your production.

The RAG study provided a lot of time-management tips from top advisors. First, many felt they were extremely hard workers in their early years. They spent a lot of time simply trying to get in front of prospects. They admitted that they really didn't know much about time management and delegation, and that they just wanted to make it. Fear of failure and a desire to succeed were all the motivation top advisors needed. They worked hard to build a client base and to earn a living, knowing that if they could do that, things would work out. And for most of these top advisors, things did.

As time went on, they learned to delegate. They hired staff, built their teams, and spent 70 percent or more of their time doing the very things that we have been talking about in this chapter: focusing on relationships, emphasizing marketing, developing niches, and developing professional referral networks. They go to fundraisers, hold client-appreciation events, and attend networking events. Most importantly, they spend more than 50 percent of their time in front of clients and prospects.

So look back on the 11 characteristics of and methods used by top advisors and decide which strategies you can incorporate into your business immediately. Decide now to get more involved in your community and with charities. Determine what you will do to become more effective and efficient. There is a whole world waiting for you, but you must act now.

Building an Effective Team

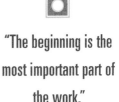

I learned a very valuable lesson in my first month as managing partner of my agency in August 1977. I was mowing my lawn on a Saturday morning when my neighbor, a successful businessman, stopped in my driveway on the way to his office. I was 30 years old, and he was much older than I was, so he felt comfortable giving me advice. He asked me politely, "Do you have anything you can do at your office that would make you more than $30 this morning?" I was puzzled by the question. Then he pointed across the street to his house, where three men were cutting his grass and trimming the edges. He said, "That's what I pay those three guys to do my yard work so that I can go to the office and get other tasks done that will pay me a lot more."

I walked across the street to his house and hired the landscaping crew. It cost only $26 for them to mow my smaller lawn. After that, I started working Saturday mornings whenever possible. If I stayed home, lying on the couch, I would be spending money, but if I went to the office and did my real job, I was investing money.

That is what we are doing when we hire staff. We are investing money.

While our staff members are doing other tasks, we are out seeing people and doing other high-level work. Can a good staff person help you make another $50,000 of premium? I believe that is the minimum they will contribute if you spend more of your time in front of prospects and clients. Remember: Have the lowest-paid person capable of doing the task do the task. And not only are staff members capable of doing the tasks you assign to them, in many cases they will execute them far better than you could.

In Chapter Five, we learned about the importance of the team. People never succeed alone; they only fail alone. That's why top advisors build a vertical team of self-starters (A+ or A team members) to support them — so

When we hire staff, we are investing money.

they can spend more time in front of clients and less time performing administrative functions.

In this chapter, we'll look at some staffing considerations, including when you should hire staff, how many people you should hire, how much you should pay them, why you should empower your team to create a "wow" experience for clients, and the ideal characteristics of an assistant.

First, though, we'll look back at the way it was 44 years ago, when I entered this great industry.

Staffing: Then vs. Now

In 1968, when I was a college intern, I worked with many reps who had no assistants. They made 10 to 15 dials a day, reached five to 10 people on the phone, and set up three to five appointments. There was no voice mail and no caller ID. Generally, a secretary would politely put you through to Mr. Big.

There were no calculators or computers, and reps did policy audits with paper and pencil. We did have access to a computerized planning tool. We would fill in the boxes with a No. 2 pencil, put the form in an envelope with $2 cash, and send it to the home office to be processed. We would expect to see it back in a week to 10 days. We always scheduled the closing appointment at least two weeks in the future. When the form came back, we would cut out red, green, and yellow acetate film to fill in the graphs. And back then, there was no compliance. All we sold was good old-fashioned whole life, and we didn't need compliance to do that.

Back then, there were a lot of reps, then called agents, who did all their own work, including filing policy status cards. They still needed to keep 60 face-to-face appointments — and, like today, not enough did. They could achieve MDRT by doing $1 million in face amount. The company-leading agent that year might have been our own John Todd, who had perhaps $3.5 million in face amount. In comparison, our 2012 leader had in excess of $200 million of face amount!

But then, like now, the top agents had staff, and the big thinkers like John Todd had substantial organizations. The reps who saw the big picture were few and far between. Many people want to praise these top reps for their sales ability, while I would contend that it's really their business-building ability for which they should be praised.

Now, let's take a look at the staff side of the business today. There are, in general, three groups of reps:

- **Reps with part-time or no staff.** This group, made up mostly of newer reps, struggles to get things done. By not hiring staff as early as possible, they get consumed doing prep work and filler tasks, which provide them with an excuse for not seeing people. This is a fatal trap. Our organization helped these reps by providing staff who were equipped to do all the prep work. That left a rep with only two things to do: be at an appointment or fighting like hell to get one.

- **Reps who have one staff member.** These reps usually hire someone after they've been in the business for a year or so. It's usually a challenge for reps to stay out of the way of their new assistants. Our office was always there to help train new assistants.

- **Reps who have more than one staff member.** These reps are functioning at very high levels. They leave all the prep work and administrative tasks to their team members. This allows them to spend most of their time going out on appointments and getting in front of people.

As I mentioned, the best thing I have ever heard a rep say when talking about how he built his staff of five people was that, when the time came to hire a second staff person, he told his assistant to hire an assistant.

Think about that. He was giving his assistant an opportunity to grow by hiring someone to help her. By allowing her to hire someone with complementary skills, he was giving her a chance to find someone to do the things she didn't like to do or didn't do well. In the process, he was also creating a system whereby his assistant would manage the new staff member. He wouldn't have the added responsibility. What a great idea!

When Should You Hire Staff?

One of the most important decisions a financial representative must make is when to hire staff.

In a perfect world, a rep would come into this business and hire a staff person on day one. But because we don't launch our businesses that way, we have to find other solutions. The time to hire staff is well before you feel you can afford to do so. If you wait until you feel you can afford it, it's too late. Depending on the support services your firm provides, a new rep should have at least part-time help six to 12 months into the business.

Let's consider a few other occupations as we look at this decision.

Consider a person who wants to open a restaurant, for instance. He has to buy equipment, sign a lease, build out the space, and hire staff, all before he cooks his first meal. Then, heavily borrowed, he opens the doors and hopes. He hopes people will come in. He hopes people will say good things about the restaurant to their friends. He hopes he can make it before his start-up money runs out. He works 80 or 90 hours a week, including most weekends and holidays. And he probably can't expect to make a real profit for up to three years.

Now, let's look at an accountant. Assuming that she wants what we have, which is the right to be in business for ourselves, she, too, goes into start-up mode. She leases a small space, hires at least one staff person, buys computers, copier machines, a microwave, and a coffeemaker, and opens the doors. Then she calls on friends and relatives, hoping to prepare some tax returns, calculate the monthly financials for small businesses, or offer bill-paying services. She works hard to get referrals, makes cold calls, and sends out direct-mail campaigns to attract clients.

She may make enough in the first year to pay the business bills. In the second year, she may make enough to pay her personal bills, and in the third year, she may actually make a profit. By then, if the accountant is truly successful, it will be time for her to expand her work space and hire more help. If she does a great job, her clients will refer her to their friends, and over time, she will spend more and more time with her ideal clients.

People who want the privilege of being in business for themselves must pay a price, and that price is always paid in advance. The difference for those of us in this industry is that we don't have to put up a lot of cash to get started.

Unlike the restaurant owner, we don't have to wait for customers to find us; we can find them. Like the accountant, we can prospect for clients, but we don't have to charge fees that limit our income. We can prospect for clients who can afford a lot of what we offer, and because of this, our income potential is truly unlimited.

How Many Staff Members Should You Hire?

Reps often ask me how many people they should hire. The answer: more than you think, if you can use your staff appropriately. Your staff members should be full time, work 40 hours per week, and start as soon as possible.

If you believe the key to long-term success is 100 or more lives and 50 new clients per year, then staffing is vital. Every rep who commits to building a business must have at least one extremely competent staff member, preferably more.

If you have plateaued, it's probably time to hire more staff members — maybe a second or even a third. In these times of complexity, compliance, and computers, having a qualified staff person is as important as having an automobile.

If you have plateaued, it's probably time to hire more staff.

My advice: Start thinking like the business-person you think you are. Start thinking like you have $100,000 invested in your business. Begin to think like a person driven to achieve the Bountiful Life.

One rep I know has seven staff members who each spend at least 40 hours a week work-ing to build his business. That's 280 hours per week. Throw in at least 20 hours for the rep, and there are 300 hours per week of effort going into building his business and wealth. What a fabulous way to work. He gets to do the things he likes to do best, and he has a group of talented people taking care of all the rest.

The Understaffed Rep: Part Time Isn't Enough

Many reps try to get by with a part-time assistant by dividing the assis-tant's time with a colleague. This is a pitfall. The half-staffed agent is destined to be mediocre at best.

The part-time cycle goes like this. The rep opens cases, does all the prep work, closes cases, arranges medicals, gets busy, and fails to pros-pect or open cases during this period. Once the policies are delivered, the cycle begins again. This results in long sales cycles that kill cash flow *and* morale. The peaks and valleys of this sales cycle feature up-and-down income, which is no fun at all.

It is impossible to write 100 lives and make MDRT without a compe-tent full-time associate financial representative. As your clientele grows, the service work grows. Soon the full-time associate financial rep is swamped. Not wanting to invest more in his or her business, the rep begins to help out with the service work, and the cycle of destruction begins again. *Hire the help you need so you can get in front of more prospects.*

Paying Your Staff Members' Salaries

A rep's expense allowance is for new business to offset the acquisition cost of new clients. The allowance is designed to pay staff, not to pay your-self more. This is an easy mistake to make. If you run your business like a mom-and-pop grocery store, it will look like a mom-and-pop grocery store. And make no mistake, premature retrogression will set in early, meaning that you will peak early in your career. The faster you write business, the faster you will reach premature retrogression if you do not hire more staff. You will peak early, and the business will seem harder to you.

One of my favorite sayings is, "The leader builds the organization, and the organization builds the business." While building a business is never easy, building an organization first will help make it easier. Abandon the idea that one staff member is enough. Start thinking about adding staff as a way to keep growing your business.

Let's say you need to pay a staff person between $30,000 and $50,000 per year. With that extra help, you probably could do $100,000 more in premium. That means you'll pay for the staff member's salary within six months. Then you will have an increase in your renewals roughly equal to first-year commissions accrued to your renewal account. That's practically a dollar-for-dollar return on your investment.

> Hire good people, and get out of their way. Use the time they free up to see more prospects and clients.

Once you hire your staff members, be aware that you will never get ahead by watching them work. Hire good people, and get out of their way. Use the time that they free up for you to see more prospects and clients. And encourage your staff to participate in online sales training. These resources help reps retain key people, so take full advantage of them.

Today we have a lot more tools in our toolbox. We have numerous financial products, more to learn, more to comply with, more complexity, and more opportunity. Don't get saddled down doing everything yourself or with just one staff member. Moving your business forward will require you to hire quality people. You will never succeed beyond the level of your least talented staff member. Remember, it's a team effort.

Empower Your Team to Create a "Wow" Experience

In February 2011, I was serving as president of my company's Managing Partners Association and attended the Southern Regional Meeting in Orlando. It was a great meeting, and spirits were high as our company continued its strong performance. But when you say "Orlando" in my house, what that means, to my grandchildren at least, is a trip to the Walt Disney World Resort. So the three oldest grandkids made the trip to Orlando with me to allow me to perform my grandfatherly duties: taking them to Disney World. (My son Peter's three children are still a little too young to go, so that leaves me something to look forward to in retirement.)

If you know me, you know that I am not a fan of crowds and lines. We were at Disney World over Presidents' Day weekend. The theme park averages 45,000 visitors per day, but that Saturday it felt like 250,000. Lines were long. The wait to get onto a ride averaged 50 to 80 minutes, and there was barely a place to stand, let alone sit. But amid all the confusion and crowding, there were a lot of smiling faces, and people were getting along.

I began to think about the park's operation. It's pretty incredible how they keep thousands of very courteous employees working hard at "making dreams come true." Disney World embodies the "wow" factor.

Our business is obviously very different from Disney World, but there are some similarities. I thought about the vision it took to create such a masterpiece. Nothing is left to chance at Disney, and everything is perfectly orchestrated.

What is your vision, and what are your carefully orchestrated plans to create a "wow" experience for your clients?

Many years ago, Walt Disney had a vision. There were no parks, no bands, and no characters — there was no money, either. All of those details had to be worked out. But once a plan is in place, once you have the strategic direction of your business, the tactical plan will come.

What is your vision, and what are your carefully orchestrated plans to create a "wow" experience for your clients?

The tactical aspects are around the service you provide. What is your plan, and what are the duties of your staff? Are they cast members, like Disney's are? In other words, do they have a role to play, or do they just show up and handle paperwork? Are they part of the experience? Do they know their lines?

At Disney, no job is too big or too small. I saw managers walking around with litter grabbers in their hands, picking up garbage as they moved around the park. Cleanliness is everyone's job. It's a matter of pride. Do you take pride in your work space? Does it represent who you want to be? This includes the "uniforms" we wear. We should dress in a professional and distinguished manner, appropriate for providing a "wow" experience for clients. Everyone at Disney looked ready for the performance. I have no doubt that they relax after hours, just not on the job.

And the performers at Disney — the characters and dancers — give it their all. They have to be "on" all the time because they never know when a child is about to make a memory. The dancers jump, kick, and twirl as if it were a command performance. There is a precision in all they do. Can you say the same?

As the day wore on, my wife, Bea, looked at the crowds and asked a simple, rhetorical question: "What recession?" She was right — there seemed to be no recession, judging from the crowds at Disney World. That got me thinking about our business again. It greatly upsets me to know that our industry has let 35 million households go without buying life insurance. Then I wondered whether it might be possible that one-third of the people at the Disney park could have no life insurance, yet could spend $85 per person for a one-day ticket, $5 for each Coke, and hundreds of dollars on souvenirs? It's obvious that the families in the park loved their family members. I watched parents hug their children, laugh with them, and wipe their noses. But what happens if they are no longer around to do those things? What about the money the family will need to stay in their home? What about their children's college education?

The Beatles sang, "Money can't buy me love." And that's true. But it does afford you choices. It makes one of the toughest times in your life just a little easier. It allows you to focus on your family's needs and wants without their having to work to pay bills or ask for aid.

As I moved about the park, I couldn't help but wonder how many of these people had escaped the care of a good financial representative to whom they said, "Sorry, we can't afford it." Can't afford it? At my best estimate, it must cost a family of four no less than $3,000 to vacation at Disney World for two to three days, which is a typical stay. Even one day at the park, if you are within driving distance, might cost $500 to $1,000. And yet many would say they can't afford life insurance.

Whenever you feel like there aren't any prospects out there, remember that one in three people have no coverage. Just keep asking the simple question, "Would you have any objection to talking to me about your life insurance program sometime?"

As we were leaving the park, my four-year-old grandson vomited on Main Street, where thousands of people were walking to leave the park. My daughter scrambled to help Teddy, who was a mess. He had just been handed a stuffed Mickey Mouse doll to take home. That was trashed. In the midst of the chaos, a Disney cast member came up to us and asked if he could help. His job was to take photos of people as they walked down Main Street. Moments later, the balloon lady came over, and my daughter asked if she could call someone to clean up the mess on Main Street. She replied, "We are already working on that."

Then the photographer, noticing the ruined Mickey doll, asked if we had just bought it, and we answered yes. He left his post on the street, took my son-in-law with him, and called the manager to explain the problem. Moments later, the manager authorized him to give us a replacement doll and a new shirt for Teddy, at no cost.

With thousands of people everywhere and thousands of cast members doing their jobs, they still knew exactly what to do if someone was in distress. Does your team have a plan like that? Do you know exactly what to do? Are your cast members empowered to help people, to create a "wow" experience like they do at Disney? If not, sit down with them and come up with ways to help your clients have a "wow" experience that all of your team members contribute to. If you do so, your clients will probably remain loyal and also refer you to their friends, family members, and colleagues.

A Rep's Toughest Job

Hiring a great assistant is every rep's dream. The right person can make a huge difference. There is no telling the number of hours that reps waste on selecting and training assistants. To get the best assistant to meet your needs, you need to be willing to ask the tough questions. Doing so is among the most important investments of time and money you'll ever make.

It's important to know what you are looking for. So here's a list of 10 characteristics of the ideal candidate — the assistant who you should be looking for. A person who:

- Shows up early every day and stays late
- Never takes an unscheduled day off
- Never goes home until the work is done
- Studies all the latest techniques and keeps up on new courses and programs
- Leaves all personal issues at home and never brings them to work
- Has a positive attitude, smiles, and brightens the office all day long
- Understands your compensation plan and takes advantage of all bonus opportunities
- Studies and follows all proven methods for success
- Never spends time talking and gossiping with co-workers

- Believes that easy jobs don't pay much

- Works hard at increasing his or her value to the organization

Can you imagine coming to work every day and working with someone like this person? Your productivity would go through the roof!

*Well, I have a surprise for you. That person should be **you!***

The toughest part of your job is managing yourself, not managing staff. Look in the mirror each morning, and have a discussion with yourself. As the boss, would you keep you around? As I look back on my 40-plus years in this business, I can think of some great people who just could not manage themselves. That shortcoming is the root of their failure. Some will always perform at a higher level than others, but no one should fail because they lack the qualities I just listed.

> Your behavior establishes the standard — the moral code, the work ethic, the desire to help others. So decide on the person you want to be, and then act accordingly.

Now go back over these questions keeping yourself in mind. Are you a model of the person you want working for you? Do you always arrive early? Do you work late? Do you take days off only with good reason? Do you leave only after the work is done? Do you plan ahead and anticipate your work load and problems? Do you keep up with your studies? Are you a lifelong learner? Do you leave personal issues at home? Do you understand your compensation plan and take advantage of all bonus opportunities? Do you follow the proven method for success that you have been taught? Do you avoid talking and gossiping with colleagues during work time? Do you really believe that easy jobs don't pay much, and thus work hard at making your job pay well?

Before you blame anyone for your lack of results, ask yourself if you embody these 10 characteristics. Answer honestly, and then get to work being the best you can be. You may need to fire that person in the mirror and hire a new one in the morning.

If you behave like the person described above, you will be surprised at how closely your assistant(s) will follow suit. Your behavior establishes the standard — the moral code, the work ethic, the desire to help others. So decide on the person you want to be, and then act accordingly.

(And yes, you should still look for these same characteristics in the people you hire.)

Gaining Trust With Clients

Scottish author, poet, and minister George MacDonald said, "To be trusted is a greater compliment than to be loved." I believe this is true, and in our business, building trust among clients is critical to our ability to succeed.

"The soul never thinks without a picture."

—Aristotle

We hear a lot about trust these days. Our society is still wounded by the economic downturn and by the fraud that led to its collapse. Barely a day goes by that we don't hear about foreclosures, insider trading, and scandals. A 2010 MDRT study reported that 85 percent of consumers found it more difficult to trust financial advisors than they did five years prior in 2005.[23]

A Lack of Trust Is an Opportunity

Let's start with a definition of trust. *Trust is the belief that someone or something is reliable, good, honest, and effective.* It is the generalized expectation held by an individual that the word of another can be relied on. You can imagine how hard it would be for us to do business with someone who cannot trust us. Mistrust and skepticism are rampant in our culture right now. And rightly so. There are myriad reasons not to trust a variety of institutions and people — whether it is the government, politicians, sports figures, or the numerous unscrupulous people in financial services, Bernie Madoff among them, who were uncovered and brought to justice.

What is a person to think? When asked, 74 percent of consumers said Madoff is the norm in the financial world. Only 25 percent said banks are honest and trustworthy. It may take years to regain the consumers' trust. The dishonest acts of a few provoke distrust in general.

On the other hand, we know there are people who want to buy our products, and they are looking for someone they can trust. That is indeed a great opportunity, but betrayal is everywhere. Playwright Tennessee

---

[23] *Generational Finance Confidence Study*, Million Dollar Round Table, 2010. http://www.mdrt.org/UserFiles/File/MDRTGFCReport_October2010.pdf, Accessed December 2013.

Williams said, "We have to distrust each other. It is our only defense against betrayal." That's a pretty negative worldview, but a great many people would agree with it.

In 2010, I had the opportunity to attend the LIMRA Distribution Conference. A main-platform topic that got my attention was the lack of trust consumers have in the people and institutions around them. This can be a real problem for us if we cannot win the trust of the people we call on and with whom we hope to work. But it can also be a huge opportunity for us if we can learn to effectively build trust with people.

I have spoken for years about the phenomenon of phoning for appointments. From our most veteran advisor to our youngest rep, for every two referrals we speak to on the phone, we get one appointment. Why does that happen? Don't they have anything better to do than sit around and talk to a financial representative? Do they need company in their homes at night while the kids are running around? Of course not. It's because they want to take care of needs they know they have, and they are looking for someone to guide them. So when you show up, why don't they just tell you all their problems and buy a product? It's because in the first meeting, you don't interview them — they interview you! The first meeting is when they are determining if they think you are sincere, honest, and trustworthy.

This can be our greatest opportunity if we can learn to connect with people in a genuine way. Why do some reps write so many lives and new clients while others who seem to be of similar work ethic and knowledge just can't get it done? I believe it is because some people are seen as more sincere, honest, and trustworthy than others.

You never get a second chance to make a first impression. I knew everyone in my organization was trustworthy, or they wouldn't have been invited to join it in the first place. But there are some things that reps need to think about and implement in their approach that can make the best of them even better trust builders and can help those who are not naturals at trust building become much better. Start by making the most of every opportunity.

Many years ago at an MDRT meeting, a rep talked about a sales call he had made. The appointment went along very well as he explained how life insurance worked. However, as the agent moved to the close, the prospect took a surprise position. He told the agent that while everything he said made sense, he was a very religious man and believed deeply in God and His love for man. Therefore, he told the agent, he believed that God would take care of his family in the event of his death.

The agent was exasperated by this response. Challenging the prospect to no avail, he finally asked how he thought God would provide this care.

The prospect said he wasn't sure, but knew God would send someone to him. Seeing his opportunity, the agent then asked, "Do you think there is any chance God sent me here tonight?" The stunned prospect responded, "Where do I sign?"

Four Pillars of Trust

I love LIMRA research because the organization can ask people questions we cannot. LIMRA researchers have studied consumer trust extensively. They listen to consumers and then match their responses with the thinking of some very bright people.

> The best reps are almost teacher-like when they present information to a prospect. They always check for understanding and agreement along the way, and they always explain everything in a self-effacing manner.

Here is what we know: Consumers want financial advice, but they need to be able to understand it. The best reps I know are almost teacher-like when they present information to a prospect. They always check for understanding and agreement along the way. They never assume someone else knows what they know, and they always explain everything in a self-effacing manner. They would never embarrass a person because he or she may not know something about our products. No one likes being made to feel stupid.

There are four key pillars of trust, and anyone in this business must not only know them but also be able to talk about them:

- **Competency. Do I trust that you know what you are doing?** Of the four pillars, this one is the least important, according to LIMRA's research, because the consumer assumes you know what you are doing and maintains that opinion until you prove otherwise. Your commitment to lifelong learning is the best way to avoid proving otherwise.

- **Dependability. Do I think you will do what you say?** This pillar demonstrates why it's important to follow up with clients and prospects: You want your clients to think of you as dependable. Always do what you say you will. Clients will leave, often without telling you, if you do not. You may not get a second chance to keep a promise. That is what trust is about. Send thank-you notes and discovery agreements to prove that you follow up.

- **Integrity. Do I trust that you will not steal from me?** Many people have the attitude of "I will start letting my guard down when people stop giving me reasons to keep it up." People like anecdotes because they can relate to them. Learn to share true stories that help people understand that you would never steal from them or give them bad advice. Tell them a story of what another client said about how honest and sound your advice was for them.

- **Benevolence. Do I trust that you will take care of me?** Again, tell your prospects how you take care of your clients. Tell them about the services you provide dependably, and tell them you are committed to delivering those services for many years to come.

Consumers want to buy, and they are looking for an advisor they can keep.

Remember, consumers want to buy, and they are looking for an advisor they can keep.

They don't want to go through the process of choosing an advisor over and over again. Consumers want to meet their advisor by way of a referral. If you can't ask your clients for referrals in this environment, it's tantamount to admitting you haven't done a good job for them. Their friends and relatives are telling every researcher they can find that they want to be referred to a trusted advisor. Tell them with conviction that you are that person.

Tell them, looking straight in their eyes, that you are competent, dependable, and of high integrity and that you will take care of them. If you can do that, you will receive all the referrals you need, and acquiring new clients will be easy. People don't care how much you know until they know how much you care.

Now more than ever, because of the state of our economy, we need to work on being trusted and trustworthy. The trustworthy salesperson can thrive in today's less trusting environment. The more people mistrust, the more they crave someone to trust. It's as if everyone is looking for salvation. The big payoff for building trust is not only a lasting relationship with your client, but also numerous referrals to people they know.

Trust Is Fragile

In *The Magic of Thinking Big*, Dr. David J. Schwartz, a world-renowned authority on motivation, discussed trust.

Trust is a feeling. It's fragile. It takes time and effort to build trust but only an instant to destroy it. The most fundamental approach to building relationships of trust is to recognize that most prospects have one thing in common: the need to be appreciated and to feel important.

Dr. Schwartz says reps should provide "ego food" to their prospects. "Ego food" comes in five "brands." That is, these are five ways you can feed your prospects' egos:

- Compliment the prospect's appearance.

- Congratulate him or her on specific achievements.

- Recognize his or her family members, who they are, or what they have done.

- Make your prospects look smart — because they are!

- Acknowledge possessions in which the prospect takes pride.

  I have added a few "ego food" supplements of my own to the list:

- Use the prospect's name regularly and be certain of its pronunciation.

- Ask for the prospect's advice and opinion.

- Be authentic in all of your expressions. This builds belief and credibility, which leads to trust.

- Above all, be trustworthy!

Two other trust building strategies you'll want to employ are *consistency* and *information sharing*. First, prospects tend to trust sales professionals who are consistent and predictable in their behavior. Such characteristics and behaviors as punctuality, returning telephone calls, and making good on promises are some of the ways in which you will be measured. Second, referring business to prospects or clients or sharing information that will help them in their work in some way is a sure-fire means of building trust.

Relationships make the world go 'round. While your prospects are interested in insurance and investments, they are also human and social. Your prospects may claim to be motivated by intellect alone, but the professional and wise salesperson knows that people run on both logic and emotion. You must appeal to both.

How Trust Entered the Realm of Agent/Advisor Training

Life insurance sales training has gone through many changes since I came into the business 44 years ago.

This training is different from other types of sales training because of the unique nature of the product of life insurance. Not only is life insurance an intangible product, it is also one that addresses a topic most people know is inevitable but would prefer not to think about: death and dying.

To be successful in the life insurance business, we have to be good at helping people see the benefits of owning life insurance. They can't drive it, drink it, or dote on it. The only way you can understand how it will make you feel is to delve deep into your sense of responsibility.

> Prospects for life insurance have to trust the agent or advisor they work with if they are to truly achieve peace of mind. Remember, they won't be here to see how things went. There are no do-overs.

Prospects for life insurance have to trust the agent or advisor they work with if they are to feel they can truly achieve peace of mind. Remember, they won't be here to see how things went. There are no do-overs.

In 1968, my first year in this business, life insurance agent training was just beginning to use a needs-based approach. The days of product pushers were coming to an end as Baby Boomers were beginning to start families. Young Boomers wanted planning, and they needed more than just the product of the week. Companies responded to the changing demographics by developing features like family income riders to attach to traditional whole life products. Family plans started to pop up so that people could insure everyone in the family with some level of coverage.

That was also the time when we began to understand more about relationship building. Life insurance agent training began to address the soft skills of selling, which include asking questions and listening. It was breakthrough thinking at the time. Agents began to think about the sales process as two steps instead of one. The first step was to take down the facts, and the second step was to go back and show the proposal to the prospect. This was quite different from the single meeting or "one and done" approach.

But by the early 1980s, the industry lost its way. Computers allowed creative teams to design new and different products. A new policy series could be built and released in a matter of months. The economy was booming, people were inspired, and rate-of-return selling became the craze. Variable products and universal life chassis allowed companies to talk about stock market returns, and personal selling was lost. Rate of return was king.

Then the boom ended. It actually took two busts to do it. First we had the dot-com bust, and then we had the real estate bust. Add to that a fair amount of distrust, and the sale of life insurance was in trouble. If agents couldn't sell rate of return, what were they to do? Agents started leaving the business. Then compliance became a necessary part of the business, and it drove off even more agents. Life insurance ownership reached an all-time low among Americans.

Needs-Based Selling

Forty years ago, when I was new to this business, trust flourished. People were not as skeptical as they are today. They assumed you were telling them the truth. You could gain the highest level of trust by doing business with someone from your church, fraternity, or civic organization (like the Rotary Club), or with someone with whom you shared ethnic origins.

But it's different today. The key to success in the 21st century will be to learn to communicate effectively to bridge the trust gap.

Life insurance selling in the 21st century is needs-based. It is focused on the person, not the product. It helps people achieve peace of mind and meet their personal responsibilities.

The answer lies in understanding and using the seven behavioral economic tactics to engineer agreement. As you will learn, the seven tactics, which are presented in Chapter 9, can increase the likelihood of buying by 29 percent.[24]

The Psychology of the Consumer

Understanding the psychology of the consumer is more important than ever. LIMRA has studied consumers to find out why they don't buy and hears repeatedly that people are confused and overwhelmed and just don't know what or whom to believe. A high percentage of consumers said they would appreciate a referral to an advisor from a friend as a way to gain trust.

LIMRA conducted consumer focus groups to hear firsthand what was on their minds.[25] During interviews, they obtained continuous feedback so they could study reactions during the interviews. The findings showed that when an interview was conducted using behavioral economic tactics, people were 29 percent more likely to buy. Apply that increase to Al

---

[24] The seven behavioral economic tactics form the basis for the *Trustworthy Selling* program, available from HPN at www.hoopis.com.

[25] James O. Mitchell, *Improving Sales Presentations Using Choice Architecture to Influence Decisions* (Windsor, Conn.: LIMRA, 2009).

Granum's 10:3:1 formula (10 dials will gain you three conversations and one appointment), and think about the results. Awesome!

Seventy percent of consumers say they decide if they can trust an advisor in the first few minutes of a meeting and know for certain by the end of the first meeting. Think how important those first few minutes with a prospect are. Think about how important your appearance is. Knowing that makes me feel good about insisting for 40 years that reps wear white shirts. White shirts, the surveys report, make a person look more intelligent and more professional. It's why in 35 years as a managing partner I never came to the office in anything but a white shirt and suit. I recognized early on that I needed all the help I could get.

What if, even after listening to your compelling presentation, someone doesn't want to buy life insurance? Let them know that you understand how they are feeling. Say something like, "Mr./Ms. Prospect, our company belongs to an industry association that does research for us. They have studied consumers and their attitudes about buying financial products. They tell us that consumers are confused and overwhelmed and that they lack trust in advisors. I want you to know that, as we proceed, I am aware of this and will do my absolute best to help you clear up any potential misunderstandings and work hard to gain your trust." It's a genuine statement, and you'll feel good making it. Plus, there is great power in beginning the discussion that way, so try it.

The Greek philosopher Euripides said, "A bad beginning makes a bad ending." Clients want to be understood. They want you to get to know them.

Trust is about character. You cannot manufacture trust. You must simply be trustworthy to get ahead in life. But you can learn how to communicate your character and your trustworthiness. As another great Greek philosopher, Heraclitus, said, "A man's character is his fate." And Solon, a Greek statesman, said, "Put more trust in nobility of character than in an oath."

Earlier, I mentioned that in the trust building model, competency is the least important of the four factors of trust — consumers say they assume you are competent until you prove otherwise. My hope is that we as an industry can get back to the point where trust itself is assumed, until we prove otherwise — because we will have earned it.

Seizing Opportunity During Times of Economic Uncertainty

In 2010, the Business Cycle Dating Committee of the National Bureau of Economic Research reported that the most recent recession, which began in December 2007, officially ended in June 2009. This official end date makes the most recent downturn the longest since World War II and confirms what many had suspected — that the 2007–09 recession was the deepest on record since the Great Depression, at least in terms of job losses.[26]

"Twice and thrice over, as they say, good is it to repeat and review what is good."

—Plato

The recession did tremendous damage to Americans' finances. *The Washington Post* reported in June 2012 that the recent recession wiped out nearly two decades of Americans' wealth, with middle-class families bearing the brunt of the decline. The Federal Reserve said the median net worth of families plunged by 39 percent in just three years, from $126,400 in 2007 to $77,300 in 2010. That put Americans roughly on par with where they were in 1992.[27]

Every hardship presents opportunity for someone. The economic downturn of the past few years has presented our industry with incredible opportunity to help people recognize how critical it is to save money, protect their assets, and insure their lives.

In this economy, there are plenty of people who are not doing well financially, but there are some who are doing well despite the economic downturn. Both groups present huge opportunities for reps in the financial planning business. For people in the first category, accumulating wealth is a challenge, and we can help. For those in the second category, asset protection is critical, and we can help with that, too. Now is the best time to position ourselves as experts in financial security.

---

[26] Business Cycle Dating Committee, National Bureau of Economic Research, September 20, 2010, accessed June 10, 2012, http://www.nber.org/cycles/sept2010.html.

[27] Ylan Q. Mui, "Americans Saw Wealth Plummet 40 Percent from 2007 to 2010, Federal Reserve Says," washingtonpost.com, last updated June 11, 2012, accessed June 12, 2012, http://www.washingtonpost.com/business/economy/fed-americans-wealth-dropped-40-percent/2012/06/11/gJQAlIsCVV_story.html?tid=pm_pop.

Now is the best time to position ourselves as experts in financial security.

The Boomers Are in Trouble

Retirement planning tops all of the surveys when it comes to the priorities on people's minds. For many consumers, retirement planning is synonymous with accumulation of assets. That is why I recommend that you discuss this subject with everyone with whom you meet.

The Baby Boomers, of course, will be the first to require retirement planning. As of this writing, the youngest of them are turning 50 while the oldest are turning 68 at the rate of 10,000 per day. Poor preparation and a bad economy have devastated what they managed to accumulate. According to a recent survey by investment advisors Financial Engines, nearly half of all Boomers fear their retirement will result in poverty. They are terrified that they will outlive their retirement savings.

Think about the issues they face: a stock market crash, real estate values making an anemic recovery in most areas of the country, low interest rates (which are only good from the point of view of someone seeking a loan), and a recession and its aftermath. In the Financial Engines survey, more than half of Boomers expressed uncertainty about their retirement future. And the LIMRA research indicates that nearly half of all Baby Boomers are distrustful of financial services and insurance firms. More than one-third said they did not feel comfortable about making financial decisions.

More than 47 percent of Baby Boomers are at risk of running short of money in retirement, according to the 2010 Retirement Readiness Ratings by the Employee Benefit Research Institute. One in four workers exhausted all of their savings during the recession.

Baby Boomers need our financial advice, and they are seeking financial advisors. IBISWorld's 2012 report about our industry's outlook said, "A long-term trend in the industry's favor is the aging of the U.S. population. The Baby Boomer generation, the largest generation in U.S. history, is starting to reach retirement age. As they approach retirement, their demand for financial planning services will increase, intensifying demand industry-wide."[28]

In what I have called the Golden Age of Financial Services, this is one of the biggest nuggets. The Baby Boomer market is huge and presents a significant opportunity for us.

---

[28] "Financial Planning and Advice in the U.S.," IBISWorld, accessed June 4, 2012, http://www.ibisworld.com/industry/default.aspx?indid=1316.

IBISWorld also projected that the retirement planning field would grow by nearly 134 percent and named it the second fastest-growing industry from 2010 to 2019.[29]

Reps can help those Boomers facing financial uncertainty and trouble by taking on the mission and becoming advocates for retirement savings. You have all the financial tools you need to help people prepare for their future in this economy. Even the youngest of prospects know they need to start the accumulation process as soon as possible. You need to become an expert in personal planning and needs analysis for retirement.

We can make a difference every day. We can do something about this looming crisis in America. We can help keep America strong. We can help people retire with dignity. My father once told me something that I will never forget: "Harry, remember this — the difference between an old man and an elderly gentleman is his income." And while he lived to be 90, and my mother, who God willing will soon turn 100, they did not outlive their money. While not big spenders, they lived with dignity.

Consumers Ages 24 to 49 Are Stressed

Boomers aren't the only ones who are hurting. In March 2011, a *USA Today* Snapshot reported data based on a survey conducted by American Express of 1,253 people between the ages of 24 and 49. They were asked "How stressful is your financial situation?" Eighty-three percent responded "very or somewhat stressful." Fourteen percent said "not stressful at all," and 3 percent said they "weren't sure."

So with 83 percent of consumers ages 24 to 49 experiencing financial stress, we have to ask what exactly they are stressed about. Here are a few facts from the 2011 Employee Benefit Research Institute's Retirement Confidence Survey. First, more workers are pessimistic about their retirement future than at any time in the last two decades. The percentage who are "not at all confident about saving enough for a comfortable retirement" reached 27 percent, up from 22 percent in just one year. When combined with the 23 percent who said they are "not too confident," the total climbs to 50 percent of workers.[30]

Also, the number of workers saving for retirement declined from 60 percent the previous year to 59 percent. Forty-one percent of Americans are not saving for retirement. This represents a crisis. Consider also that 29 percent said they have less than $1,000 saved, and 56 percent said

[29] "E-commerce is the Third Fastest Growing Industry, According to Study," InternetRetailer.com, last updated December 29, 2009, accessed June 11, 2012, http://www.internetretailer.com/2009/12/29/e-commerce-is-the-third-fastest-growing-industry-according-to-s.

[30] http://www.ebri.org/pdf/surveys/rcs/2011/FS1_RCS11_Confidence_FINAL1.pdf, accessed December 12, 2013.

their savings and investments, excluding their home value, total less than $25,000. Understanding these figures will help you build trust among your prospects. Letting them know that you understand the issues in our society better positions you as part of the solution.

People simply don't know what to do, and they do not have a realistic picture of what their future holds. For example, 74 percent of workers surveyed said they may need to work in retirement, but only 23 percent of retirees say they have worked in retirement. There is a serious gap between what people think will happen and what actually happens.

LIMRA research says retirement planning is one of the most important issues on the consumer's mind. An MDRT survey confirmed this fact. Only one in six people have a retirement plan, yet we know that even people in their 20s want to discuss establishing one. The Phoenix Wealth Management Survey said planning was the most important thing on the consumer's mind. Retirement planning was first, estate planning was second, and financial planning was third. The MDRT study confirmed this by saying that across all generations, retirement planning is how people think about the accumulation phase, and financial planning is how they think about the preservation and/or distribution phase.

Talk to your prospects and clients from the start about retirement planning. Introduce the topic like this: "Mr./Ms. Prospect, surveys tell us that we have a crisis in America. The crisis is that most people are not saving enough money to provide for a comfortable retirement. My approach is to zero in on retirement as a focus and then discuss how to guard against the things that could derail your plan along the way, such as disability or death. How does that sound? Great, let's get started."

Consumers love a product they see as solving more than one problem.

We also know from LIMRA's consumer research that consumers love a product they see as solving more than one problem. Permanent life insurance falls into that category. Our clients can accumulate cash in a tax-sheltered environment, have cash for emergencies, convert cash to an annuity to provide an income they cannot outlive, and have a death benefit paid to loved ones in case they die. Don't forget a waiver-of-premium provision and some disability income coverage to go along with that permanent insurance. How about that for a flexible, multipurpose solution?

We are among the very few people who can really make a difference during this financial and retirement planning crisis. We can accept the mission of our business and improve the lives of everyone we work with, or we can focus on just making a buck and leave when it's over.

As my good friend Jim Worrell, a retired managing partner from Charlotte, North Carolina, likes to say, "My tie is my shield, and my pen is my sword. I am going to be in the fight every day to make America a better place by helping people with their financial futures."

Helping Clients Understand Their Situation

Imagine for a minute that you are 45 years old and have not done a very good job of saving money. You have two children: one in college and another a year away from going to college. You do have some funds earmarked for their education. Now it's time to think about your retirement.

If I were speaking to a prospect or client, I would put it in these terms: "Mr. Prospect, you now have 240 months left to work, earn, and save for the 240 months you're expected to live in retirement without an earned income."

While 20 years may seem like a long time, 240 months does not, for some reason. There are many cases in which people need a simple wake-up call. What percentage of that client's income must he now save to have 60 to 75 percent of his pre-retirement income when he stops working? The task is overwhelming. If a person lives to age 65, a life-table expectation will give a male nearly 20 years to live and a female a few more than that. It's close enough to make a point, and remember, more people than ever are expected to become centenarians.

There is a prospect out there right now who has at least one of the following questions top of mind. It is your job to provide the answers that will help that prospect better understand his or her financial situation.

- What is going on with my life insurance? Am I paying too much, too little, or do I have enough?

- I have lost a lot of money. Why? I have assets spread all over the place with too many people. What should I do?

- I can't get my arms around my financial situation. I need help. Who should I talk to?

- How do I know whether or not to trust the institutions that are now custodians of my assets?

- I never completed my buy/sell, my estate planning, or my retirement plan. Who do I call? Maybe I need a second opinion.

Clients appreciate the value that comes with a product such as cash-value life insurance that can solve more than one problem. So be sure to point out how life insurance can help with accumulation in a tax-favored way. Answer all of the "what-ifs," and demonstrate how your clients and prospects can create an income they cannot outlive.

One company executive said this in his presentation: "Savings are as important — maybe even more important — to the consumer than investing." He also said, "Cash-value insurance is about saving, not investing. We are more relevant than ever."

There is a crisis in America, but you can do something about it. Talk to everyone you meet. Make cash-value life insurance and savings your conversational hot button. Study the facts, build trust, and explain the situation to people who are overly optimistic. If you can find the inspiration to make it your calling to help Americans save more money, you can make a difference.

And you need to become an expert. Professional designations are extremely important in this trusted-advisor world. Remember, competency is one of the four components of trust. You must be able to demonstrate that you are a professional if you want to build trust.

"Save and protect" is what we need to be focused on going forward. Even if the market gains the historical average of 10 percent a year, it will still take 10 years to get back to where we were. We are in a favorable period for risk products.

Over the past few years, I have heard from reps that prospects and clients spend a lot of time talking about the economy and how bad things are. Once they get "down to business," the sale is almost never made because the "economy card" is easily played as the reason not to take action.

Instead, when the economy comes up, acknowledge it, but then say something like this: "My role is to help people like you make sure your family and financial future are OK in spite of these challenging times. Would you like to learn how I do that for people like you?" or "What I am finding is that people like you are very concerned about their financial security now and their plans for retirement down the road. Would you be interested in learning more about how I help people like you take care of those things?" These serve as opportunities to educate prospects and clients, and then make a sale, and it demonstrates that you truly care about their financial future, not just your sales numbers.

Prospect to Those Who Are Doing Well

So there are plenty of people who are not doing well whom you need to contact. But in times like these, you must also prospect to people who are doing well. There are plenty of them out there. Those people have big needs and can write big checks. Here is some prospecting language from Dr. Robert Cooper, a neuroscientist who also serves as a financial advisor to CEOs: "I get most excited when I have the chance to work with driven, motivated, highly successful people who are not ducking in these crazy times but rather want to make better choices now, to build a bridge from where they are to where they most want to be or to create their best future and the best future for everyone they care most about." Better prospecting will lead to better production.

One top advisor has shown many reps a method to generate bigger production numbers through better prospecting. For example, if you were doing around $100,000 of paid premium and wanted to do $200,000, he would say, "Can you prospect one person in the next year who can write a check for $30,000 of premium? Twice a year, every six months, can you find someone to write a check for $20,000? Once a quarter, can you find a prospect who can write a check for $10,000? Finally, can you find one person per month who can write a check for $5,000? Add that up, and that is $170,000 of paid-for premium." He used a similar example to explain how to do more than $1 million of premium. He has done it. He did more than $2 million of paid premium in 2012. Prospect for great people, and write great premium. You can do it.

Be Enthusiastic About Whole Life

LAMP 2009, the equivalent of MDRT for agency leaders and their teams, was a great meeting, and it was my 28th consecutive year to attend. The meeting was very positive and surprisingly very upbeat. Despite the recession, many good things were still going on around us.

For example, when I got on my plane to come home, there was an article in *The Wall Street Journal* about the benefits of whole life insurance. While it mentioned the difficulty of measuring rates of return, it was nothing a knowledgeable rep couldn't address. It also discussed the tax-deferred feature and pointed out that, while it allowed people to enjoy steady returns, it provided them with insurance, too — a way to both replace lost wealth and pay taxes. That's a good story.

This is a great time to be in the insurance business. This is also a good time to get back into the insurance business for those who thought the market would always go up and perhaps have lost their zest for acquiring new clients. Life insurance is there to protect you if you live too long and those you love should you die too soon — and to help take care of the hazards along the way. That's something you should be saying at least three to five times a day to clients and prospects.

We need to be enthusiastic about the benefits of permanent life insurance products. Industry legend Ben Feldman used to say, "I sell time — time to achieve your goals — and the money is there if you don't live long enough to complete them." We have forgotten these key principles. The old line was, "Do you want to save and create or create and save?" Save and create requires time to complete the plan. Life insurance is the self-completion clause. People need to buy it first.

In addition to positioning us as needed experts, another positive result of the recession has been its impact on how people will think about investing and, more importantly, about saving. We are moving from an era of entitlement to an era of thrift. This shift in attitude marks the end of the get-rich-quick age, and nothing could be more positive for us. Remember, save and protect!

So how do we get enthusiastic about our products and our job of helping people save and protect? As the great Frank Bettger said in his 1992 book *How I Raised Myself from Failure to Success in Selling*, "You must act enthusiastic to be enthusiastic!" Have you ever met an enthusiastic loser? Another way to consider this is to ask who you would rather work with, a negative person or a positive one? Finally, ask yourself, would *you* want to do business with you?

Every American has been hurt by this downturn. There is no place to hide. But as the saying goes, this, too, shall pass. In March 2009, I read that home values in the Chicago region had risen by 3.9 percent since December 2008. The good news was beginning to materialize, even then.

Choose to be a communicator, not a commiserator. Communicate a message of hope, not despair. Communicate a message of long-term value, and teach people how to save and protect. Be part of the solution, not part of the problem. It's true that if someone took your advice years ago to buy permanent insurance instead of buying term and investing or spending the difference, they would be way ahead today. Today, buying term and investing the difference is dead.

> Communicate a message of hope, not despair. Communicate a message of long-term value, and teach people how to save and protect.

Communicate that, and use the recent economic downturn to illustrate why. Turn a negative into a positive.

There's more good news. Our clients need disability insurance and long-term care insurance now more than ever before. Most have lost the ability to self-insure this risk. They need life insurance to replace lost wealth. So get out there and share the news. This is the golden era of the financial services industry, and the door to the gold is through the risk products we offer.

Training for the Race to Come

I came across the following quote by George Bacon Wood, a medical doctor in the 1800s, and couldn't help but think how appropriate it still is today: "Fortunes are not made in boom times ... that is merely the collection period. Fortunes are made in depressions or lean times, when the wise man overhauls his mind, his methods, his resources, and gets in training for the race to come."

Are you in training for the race to come?

Another top rep spoke to a full house at a company meeting in April 2009. He had a very simple adjustment for these times. Instead of 10 to 12 fact-finders per month, he was taking 15-plus, and instead of opening 30 cases a month, he was opening 40. That's it. That was his simple adjustment.

He presented some sales statistics that initially shocked me, but then I thought about them and realized that they shed light on part of the problem. Let's take a look:

- Forty-eight percent of salespeople never follow up with a prospect.

- Twenty-five percent of salespeople make a second contact and stop.

- Twelve percent of salespeople make only three contacts and stop.

- Only 10 percent of salespeople make more than three contacts.

- Two percent of sales are made on the first contact.

- Three percent of sales are made on the second contact.

- Five percent of sales are made on the third contact.

- Ten percent of sales are made on the fourth contact.

- Eighty percent of sales are made between the fifth and 12th contacts.

> If a rep takes the time to do a financial plan and needs analysis, it puts a virtual fence around the prospect for up to five years.

Think about where things might be going wrong for you. Do you suffer from call reluctance? Do you have poor follow-up? Or do you lack the right systems and structure?

In its "Opportunity to Buy" study, LIMRA bears this out by claiming that the average person buys insurance on the fifth call from a rep, and it doesn't matter which rep. Any wonder that those who follow and practice the One Card System seem to do better than those who do not? It increases the odds that you will be the fifth caller.

LIMRA also said in the same study that only 23 percent of those surveyed indicated that they had an opportunity to buy, which was defined as a single phone call from a representative. Consumers said that if a rep took the time to do a financial plan and needs analysis, it puts a virtual fence around the prospect for up to five years.

Have you been laying any fence lately? I suggest you need to do more retirement planning and needs analysis. This is what the clients want to see, and it differentiates you as a professional rather than a product pusher.

And finally, let's remember that while the logic of a plan is important, it is emotion that sells. In the battle of intellect versus emotion in selling, emotion always wins. Incorporate real-life stories and situations into your process. Emotion sells, and logic keeps the sale in force. If you aren't already training for the race to come, please start now.

Sell Planning, Not Products

The recent economic crisis has changed and will continue to change how we think about money. As management guru Peter Drucker once said, "There is a time lag between a major social, economic, or cultural event and its full impact." The age of entitlement has stepped aside to make way for the age of thrift. This is good news for our industry. The economic landscape has changed for at least the next 50 years. Become an expert on ways to save money, and you will flourish.

Imagine a prospect who listens intently to you as you describe a way for him to not only plan for retirement in 20 or 30 years, but also a way to take care of the hazards that might occur along the way. Imagine a prospect who is not hoping for or expecting a 25 percent return year after year. Imagine a prospect who wants to protect his loved ones because he knows how tough it can be out there. And imagine a prospect who isn't interested in buying term and investing the difference but instead wants to hear more about the tax-sheltered accumulation feature of cash-value life insurance so he can someday replenish the wealth he has lost.

People want a plan. They want to see how the numbers work. They are not interested in buying a product. Remember, nobody is spending. Buying a product is spending. Solving a problem is worth the investment in saving and protecting.

In 2009, five of our top six users of our financial planning tool in my agency were also our top lives writers. You owe it to every client and prospect to put them into the planning mode. This will separate you from all the product pushers and endear you to your client as someone who cares. Second, put in the time to become a master of the plan. Know it, and show it! Third, increase your use of online training programs. Now is the time to learn the things that keep you fresh.

So what do you tell your clients about your process? Try this: "My team and I create individualized integrated solutions through fact-finding and looking at the whole picture." Or this: "I help you build a bridge from where you are to where you want to be." And this: "My clients tell me they never want to feel this vulnerable again — not for their families or their businesses."

So there are three options for growth. The first one increases the quantity of activity and writes more lives. The second one increases prospects' capacity so they can afford more premium. The third one increases the quality of your process so you can close more sales. While I know all of you should increase your activity, and you know you always have to increase the quality of your prospect, it's the process that is the easiest to do. Put forth the effort, and put that virtual fence around your prospects and clients.

Consumers Have Changed

Times have changed, the way we do business has changed, and consumer attitudes and behavior have changed. The economic downturn has made its mark on us all.

Not long ago, I attended a meeting in Washington, D.C. — GAMA International's Executive Leadership Cabinet. The group is made up of home office executives and field leaders like me. Here are a few thoughts from a couple of the speakers who presented to our group.

The first, Dr. George Vredeveld, an economist and professor from the University of Cincinnati, shared his thinking on the economy: the problems, the reality, and the forecast. The causes of the recent economic meltdown are very complex, and you have probably heard them all. What I felt was interesting was his perception that the consumer has changed, at least for the foreseeable future. In a study he cited, 89 percent of consumers said they would make fewer purchases, 88 percent said they felt more frugal, and 73 percent said they want to play it safer with money.

That information alone should provide you with some talking points for your clients and prospects. The feeling is, the more severe the crisis, the more lasting the changes in attitude will be. Dr. Vredeveld felt that housing may have hit bottom and that it would take employment a much longer time to recover to prerecession levels.

Our second speaker was Jim Thomsen, executive vice president of Thrivent Financial. His remarks included a combination of his own analysis, some surveys, and a report from McKinsey and Company. His first point in describing how things have changed had to do with the way the public views the problems we face.

The surveys he shared indicated that the public blames the financial services industry for current problems. It doesn't matter whether you took TARP money or not. It doesn't matter that banks deserve most of the blame and insurance companies very little — we are all to blame, so it seems. As I mentioned earlier, this means we now have to rebuild trust. Fortunately, we have a strong and convincing story to tell, but we all must tell it. Consumers' No. 1 concern right now is whether their money is going to be safe. There is a flight to safety, and our industry can benefit from that.

Now, while the financial services companies took a hit, the people who have a financial advisor report really trusting him or her. Those who don't have an advisor said they need one who they can trust. So it's a great time to prospect with that information.

Advisors who stay in touch with their clients during these times have a tremendous reputation advantage. A survey showed that 40 percent of consumers received a proactive call from their advisor, 30 percent had to call their advisor, and 30 percent either had no advisor or were not contacted by one over the past year. I urge everyone to stay in touch with clients as often as possible. It will pay off. Or, as Jim said at our Cabinet meeting, "Don't hide under the bed."

Be bold. Tell your story about our safe haven. Do not assume that people know.

Consumers say that their behavior has changed permanently. There is a new group of savers under the age of 40. Watching what their parents have gone through has left an imprint on them. People want safe havens, and they want companies and advisors they can trust.

So here is what Jim recommended: Be bold. Tell your story about our safe haven. Do not assume that people know. Assume instead that they are one of those who blame financial institutions. Let them know we can deliver on a promise for the long haul. Show them how well good old whole life has done over the years. They are listening now, like never before.

Second, be active in the tax battle that is brewing in Washington, D.C. Support NAIFA, support AALU, and take action when asked to do so. Spread the word to family and friends.

Finally, if you want to be trusted, then you must model and demonstrate trust. Your clients need to be the center of your work universe. They always have been, but they need to know it now more than ever. Your actions and your word are paramount.

Things are getting better. Dolly Parton said, "If you want a rainbow, you've got to put up with the rain." Consumers have accepted the fact that their homes are worth less and their 401(k) accounts are worth less. There is little they have faith in right now. They have made adjustments, and they want to save and protect what they have. You can help them. Become an expert in your company and its strengths.

And keep swinging. As Hank Aaron said, "My motto was always to keep swinging. Whether I was in a slump or feeling badly or having trouble off the field, the only thing to do was keep swinging."

Change With the Times

In an October 2009 article in the *Chicago Tribune*, Treasury Secretary Timothy Geithner was credited with saying that there is a new caution in America, and he believes it's a good thing. He said that a generation of Americans had been sobered by the financial crisis, and he expected that to affect their stomach for risk for a lifetime. He believed people would save more and borrow less while preparing for a future they now realize they cannot take for granted. They will look ahead and plan for an uncertain future. People's kids are growing up with a sense of risk, and that will be helpful to them.[31]

As inspirational writer William Arthur Ward once said, "The pessimist complains about the wind, the optimist expects it to change, and the realist adjusts the sails." So how do we adjust our sails?

---

[31] http://articles.chicagotribune.com/2009-10-31/news/0910300339_1_treasury-secretary-timothy-geithner-economic-club-financial-crisis.

Many years ago, as our agency was pioneering the diversification of the financial services business with the integration of new products and services, I created the paradox of financial services, which is this: "The more diversified we become in our products and services, the more important it becomes for us to be experts in something." We knew we had to avoid being "jack-of-all-trades, master of none." So we developed a cadre of specialists. But along the way, many reps failed to figure out what their specialty would be.

I suggest that you figure out yours now so you don't miss the huge opportunity ahead of us. What are you a specialist in? What about gaining a specialty in life insurance needs, uses, and functions? Who needs life insurance? What does it do? How does it help? Now, that is a specialty people need. And how about this elevator speech: "I specialize in the needs, uses, and functions of life insurance." That sure has a nice ring to it!

What product do you know of that will offer more benefit to the user than life insurance in today's environment? Tax-favored accumulation, tax-free death benefits, and potentially an income you cannot outlive. If we had the chance to rename this product for the 21st century, what would it be? A comprehensive lifetime planning tool? Womb-to-tomb security? One check, one plan? Certainly, I am being tongue in cheek here, but you get my point.

Albert E. Gray said in his famous speech I mentioned earlier, "Our business is difficult because we call on people wanting to talk about a subject they don't want to talk about: dying." But why do that when we can instead talk about living and saving so that we can live a life of dignity, without the worries of debt and destitution?

These are clearly tough times for the 10 million to 15 million people who are unemployed. Many are losing their homes, unable to send their kids to college, and feeling an overall sense of desperation. Many worry about where their next meal will come from. People are forced to call on family and friends for help — hopefully for the short term. Yes, Geithner predicted a slow recovery marked by high joblessness, but it is also true that we will eventually recover.

Imagine a person who doesn't have a chance to recover. Suppose their spouse dies and leaves them with two or three children and no money. What will their future look like? What will they do? Might they be forced to move in with their parents? Will they be forced to sell their house and move into an apartment? Would they be forced to go on public assistance? Imagine the agony people face when they have exhausted all of their options and resources and there is simply no way out.

Albert E. Gray also had something to say about this topic: "The strength which holds you to your purpose is not your own strength, but the strength of the purpose itself." I point this out because there has not been a time like this in the last 50 years. While memories and lessons of the Great Depression took years to forget, the boom period we went through in the last 25 to 30 years has left us weak. We need to focus on the new normal.

Our purpose has to be that we help people secure a position that ensures they will never have to feel this way again. The miracle of life insurance happens every day, like our young rep's experience that turned $38 into $500,000 after just three weeks. Now is our chance to tell people that personal responsibility is the only way to assure a life of financial security. This is our purpose.

In *Life Insurance, a Textbook*, renowned scholar and professor Solomon S. Huebner, the "father of life insurance studies," made three profound statements regarding the ownership of life insurance, and they are as relevant today as they were when his life insurance textbook was first published in 1915.[32] Excuse a few old terms, as they were his.

First, he said, "Since life insurance furnishes the surest method of hedging the family against the uncertainty of life, it is essential that all who have assumed family obligations should use it as a means of protecting dependents against the want that may be occasioned by an untimely death."

Now *that* is the type of hedging that we need in this world.

Second, he said, "Emphasis should be placed on the crime of not insuring, and the finger of scorn should be pointed at any man who, although he has provided well while alive, has not seen fit to discount the uncertain future for the benefit of a dependent household."

That's short-term sacrifice for long-term gain and peace of mind. This is how providing well will be measured going forward.

Third, "Life insurance is the only means of changing uncertainty into certainty and is the opposite of gambling. He who does not insure gambles with the greatest of all chances and, if he loses, makes those dearest to him pay the forfeit." A forfeit, as used here, is defined as a penalty for a fault or mistake.

Anyone reading this needs to commit Solomon's words to memory. If you do, I can assure you these words will come through in your thinking and speaking. After 45 years in this business, these words ring truer to me today than ever before. Make them your purpose, and you will succeed. The months and years ahead will be different. Geithner said we

---

[32] *Life Insurance, a Textbook.* Solomon Stephen Huebner. 1915.

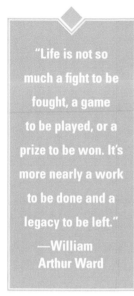

"Life is not so much a fight to be fought, a game to be played, or a prize to be won. It's more nearly a work to be done and a legacy to be left."

—William Arthur Ward

are changed for a lifetime. Your challenge is to change with the times and bring greater value to your clients than ever before.

William Arthur Ward said, "Life is not so much a fight to be fought, a game to be played, or a prize to be won. It's more nearly a work to be done and a legacy to be left." During these challenging economic times, we have more opportunity than ever to leave a legacy. Let's seize it.

The Major Market Is Our Sweet Spot

In the spring of 2010, I spent a lot of time with a very talented group of individuals: the people at LIMRA. LIMRA is dedicated to the growth and development of the insurance industry, and the organization works tirelessly to help us understand our marketplace, our consumers, our challenges, and our opportunities. The Hoopis Performance Network is a LIMRA Strategic Partner, and as such we devoted a substantial amount of time to the development of a new sales training program called *Trustworthy Selling*. This program uses LIMRA research to set the stage for the new techniques necessary to reach the consumer of the 21st century.

Anyone who thinks the consumer of today is anything like the consumer of yesterday is destined to become frustrated by spending endless hours looking for what's left of those prospects from yesterday. The 21st-century consumer has access to more information than ever before, and the skepticism created by the events of the last 12 years has given us a new consumer to deal with on a regular basis.

What follows is some insight into the financial conditions and attitudes of what I call the major market and what LIMRA refers to as the middle market. The reason I like the term "major market" is simple: It is by far the biggest segment of our population, and it represents the majority of our new clients. So while we all hope, dream, and think we target the ultra-rich, the reality of the marketplace is that the buyer earning between $50,000 and $125,000 per year is really the sweet spot for the acquisition of new clients. Here's a brief look at how they look and, more importantly, how they feel.

Middle-class Americans are financially fragile. Nearly half of all U.S. consumers say they would struggle to meet an unexpected financial burden, such as a car or home repair, or a relatively minor health-related expenditure. This is important because you need to be able to reassure prospects that they are not alone in feeling vulnerable. Your role is to help them find ways to establish a budget to fix the problem.

According to research conducted by TNS, a leader in market research, global market information, and business analysis, middle-class Americans have learned a lesson and would not revert to the use of a credit card to solve a financial hardship. Instead, they would be more likely to tap into savings or call on favors from friends or relatives to deal with it. Forty-nine percent say they would first turn to savings, 27 percent said they would turn to their families, and 21 percent said they would work over-time or get a second job.

To measure capacity for risk bearing, the TNS survey asked if consumers could come up with enough money for a major car repair in a month. The results revealed that 46 percent of U.S. consumers are unlikely to be able to find the funds, with 55 percent of 16- to 24-year-olds unable to fund such an emergency and 34 percent of 55- to 64-year-olds unable to do so. Remarkably, only 24 percent of those earning $100,000 to $149,000 would be able to find funds.

Also, LIMRA research revealed that 80 percent of middle-market households believe they are not saving enough money. People of all ages, income levels, and households are uncomfortable about their saving habits. Households that set money aside for specific financial goals are more comfortable with their overall situation than households that don't have strategies.

There is opportunity here. We need to develop the skills to become missionaries for savings. Stop thinking of just the next sale; instead, think like a person who has good advice and wisdom to spread about the importance of planning.

Knowing facts like these can help you in several ways. First, they help you see through smoke-screen objections. Realize that any given consumer you are sitting in front of most likely is not in very good financial condition. Second, realize that the consumer you are sitting in front of has probably failed to properly align income with responsibilities and needs help. Realize that consumers are probably embarrassed about their situation. Develop face-saving language to win their trust. Finally, realize

> The consumer you are sitting in front of has probably failed to properly align income with responsibilities and needs help. Develop face-saving language to win their trust.

that the guidance you offer should be needs-based and should demonstrate flexibility in solving problems. Let your client know that a relationship with you can last a lifetime.

After a financial crisis like we have gone through, where risk has been such an enormous factor, it is important to know whether consumers have any real understanding of the basic principles of financial risk. Most Americans do not.

People of all ages need our help. Lifelong learning and obtaining your CLU, ChFC, and CFP designations will be a differentiator. Many of these people know what they don't know and will be seeking an advisor who can guide them through the financial maze. Commit to learning more as fast as you can. We have the resources you need to do this. It is not all about product knowledge.

Pay attention to the changes in the marketplace. Help people achieve peace of mind. Become the kind of rep you would want to meet if you needed financial help. Adopt this mantra: "I bring to my clients the kind of advice I believe they need for the times we live in."

Yes, we are in the midst of an economic and financial crisis in America, and those of us in the financial services industry have an opportunity to be part of the solution. You might even say we have a responsibility to be part of the solution. We can take up the mission to help people save and invest wisely from an early age and help solve the prevailing retirement crisis in America. I believe we need to know as much about the crisis, if not more, than we know about our products. Remember, we don't sell products; we sell solutions to problems.

By knowing more about the dire straits many Americans have found themselves in, you can be better prepared to help your clients and prospects emerge intact from one of the most challenging periods of our history. As you set out on your path to the Bountiful Life, you can help your clients achieve the Bountiful Life, too.

For the 20 Percent Who Can Sell

If you are reading this book, you are likely among the 20 percent of people on the planet who psychologists say can sell. Within the 20 percent group, we have the usual bell-shaped curve of distribution — a lot of people in the middle do all right, a small group at one end really struggles, and a small group at the other end thrives.

Most of you reading want to be in the last group. Just remember that it's like golf: It's a repeatable swing made with a commitment to excellence. You just have to do it over and over, by the book, to make it even better. If you can do it once, you can do it again and again.

You need to think about this every day so that every day doesn't prove to be a bad swing. I see this too often — a bad day becomes another bad day. The dress and demeanor change. The signs of mediocrity begin to appear. In *Nicomachean Ethics*, Aristotle wrote, "Contemplation is the highest form of activity." Contemplate your success every day. Think about who you are and, more importantly, who you want to become.

I recently spoke to a young rep who was giving up. He is among the 20 percent of people with the talent to sell. But he said he just couldn't find enough good people to talk to. (I mean, we have only 8 million people in the Chicagoland area to call on!) And we have reps all over the country, working in towns of fewer

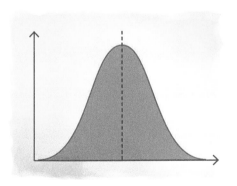

than 100,000 people, doing Top of the Table-level production. What he was really saying is, "I am not willing to work hard enough at this to get what I want out of life." If he would just intensify his efforts, focus on the positives, and work as hard as he could, he could be on the thriving end of the bell curve.

Doing It by the Book

In 2009, I was at a company meeting planning committee session. As we worked through what was to be a great program, it occurred to me that each time the committee agreed to have a certain person on the program, the same words were always spoken: "He does it by the book." I even stopped the group so I could highlight this breakthrough moment, and we all looked at each other and laughed. It's what we have always said: "Do it by the book."

The book isn't necessarily one method or the One Card System; it is having a process. The book is a system and structure that you create so that you can sell 100 lives. The idea of doing it by the book simply says that if the play worked once, it will work again and again — the repeatable swing. All you have to do is find the prospect who is enough like the first one you sold to so you can do it again. Sometimes this is referred to as "nesting," but it's really about commonality: finding people you relate to and who trust you. Don't make it more difficult than it is. Prospecting for the same people may be hard work, but then again, we know that easy jobs don't pay much.

Jack Brown, a retired managing partner, said, "Those who stay will be champions." This is true in so many ways. They will be champions in their personal lives, champions in their family lives, and champions in their communities. It's so worth the extra effort.

Heavyweight boxer Muhammad Ali, "the Greatest," said, "I hated every minute of training, but I said, 'Don't quit. Suffer now, and live the rest of your life as a champion.'" Aristotle said, "Men acquire a particular quality by constantly acting in a particular way." It's the repeatable swing again — using the same sales approach on the same type of prospect.

As you can tell, I love quotes by famous people. Perhaps because most of them weren't famous when they made the statements, but instead became famous because they practiced what they preached. The late Supreme Court Associate Justice Louis Brandeis is said to have told his daughter, "If you would only recognize that life is hard, things would be so much easier for you."

Former NFL head coach Bill Walsh said, "We have a lot of players in their first year. Some of them are also in their last year." Don't let that be you. Find your repeatable swing, and write those 100 lives.

Four Categories of Skill

In the old "Counselor Selling" program, they taught a concept based on four categories of skill.[33] These categories can be applied to salespeople.

The *conscious competents* are people who are good at what they do and know why, but they have to concentrate to get it done. *Unconscious competents* are people who have had so much practice with a skill that it has become second nature to them. *Conscious incompetents* are people who know what they do wrong, and *unconscious incompetents* are those who have no idea what they are doing wrong or why.

The conscious competents are professionals; they do their jobs well and know why. This should be everyone's goal. But the unconscious competents are the "naturals" — they are born to sell. They connect with people and get the sale. The conscious incompetents won't survive very long if they don't fix what they do wrong, and the unconscious incompetents must recognize what they do wrong before they can move forward.

Continuing to learn more about yourself and the marketplace is imperative. Simply put, those who stop getting better cease being good.

Focus on People, Not Products

Over the course of my 45 years in the industry, I have witnessed the change from a people-driven sales process to a product-driven sales process. In the 1970s, it was a product-driven sales process that needed to change to a people-driven process. It seems we have come full circle once again.

The changes in our society in the '90s and the first decade of the 21st century were "rate-of-return-oriented." It will probably be known as the Greed Period in American history, with the mantra being to take a risk, gamble, and bet that everything you invest in goes straight up. Whether it was stocks, bonds, or real estate, it was always going up. This led once again to product-driven sales instead of people-driven sales. In other words, if you could sell rate of return, the client would buy from anyone, even someone they really didn't trust, and they certainly didn't need a relationship with a sales rep. I welcome back the people-driven sales process. It is more compassionate and caring and more consistent with the kind of people I feel we attract to the business.

If you are one of those who is blessed with sales skills, you probably focus on your clients — people — regardless of what the industry or the

---

[33] *Win-Win Selling: The Original 4-Step Counselor Approach for Building Long Term Relationships With Buyers*. Wilson Learning Library. 2003.

market is doing. Yes, the products are important, but people are the most critical part of the equation.

Seven Tactics That Can Influence Prospects' Willingness to Buy

To help you achieve the repeatable swing I keep mentioning, I want to tell you about a LIMRA study called "Improving Sales Presentations: Using Choice Architecture to Influence Buying Decisions." The study specifically looked at how to present products and advice to potential buyers of insurance.

First, let's define "choice architecture." Choice architecture applies behavioral economics principles to help people make correct decisions without being influenced by potential biases. Co-authors Richard Thaler and Cass Sunstein coined the term in their 2009 book *Nudge: Improving Decisions about Health, Wealth, and Happiness.*

The premise of choice architecture is based on the following conclusions:

- People choose poorly when making financial decisions.

- The immediate context of decision making matters.

- We can improve people's decisions by controlling the features that influence those decisions.

The LIMRA research revealed that behavioral economics tactics invoke more feelings in prospects and leave a better impression on them. They give a 29 percent lift to a sales presentation. In other words, the client will be 29 percent more likely to buy when you use these tactics than when you do not use them. Learning how to use these seven tactics in your sales presentations should increase your effectiveness in very positive ways. Whether you are a newer rep or a veteran, an unconscious competent or a conscious competent, you can benefit from learning these skills. Here are the seven tactics:

1. Use personal experiences to overcome optimism.

People tend to believe that whatever it is we talk about will happen to someone else. For example, we all know we will die. Statistically, we can prove this. But some people seem to be in denial that it is going to happen to them. You need to share personal experiences involving real people to demonstrate reality to them.

People rely on others' experiences to help them decide what to do. This is known as "herding." For example, prospects in our business often assume something is good based on others' behavior, and so they follow suit. This is why referrals from friends are so important. It is not so much the introduction as it is the fact that someone else, in this case a friend, has made the decision to work with you.

Another valuable concept here is called "self-heading," which is relying on what we have done in the past to direct us in the future. Self-heading works, for instance, with existing clients who know how favorable their previous decision to buy was. This is why it's so easy to resell and cross-sell existing clients and the reason you should systematically be seeing them at least annually.

Become a storyteller to convey in a personal way what has happened to someone else and how it could affect the prospect's life and family. A story is vivid. It tells people what can happen and what they should do. By telling stories about similar people and how a situation affected them — someone who died from cancer at a young age, for instance — you will improve the way your prospect thinks about risk products. Always do it in a caring and compassionate way, not in a frightening or threatening way. If you don't have stories of your own, you can borrow them from your colleagues who have been around longer. You also can go to the Hoopis Performance Network online or visit the LIFE Foundation's website[34] and review some of their Real LIFE Stories. The videos can help you create your own way of conveying your message. Some reps even show Real LIFE Stories in their presentations.

> Become a storyteller. A story is vivid. It tells people what can happen and what they should do.

2. Avoid ambiguity.

People have a hard time making complex decisions. Did you ever stop to think that you may be preventing the buyer from making the decision to buy because you have overwhelmed him or her with information? Maybe you remember sitting in a lecture hall in college thinking, "What in the world is this professor talking about?" In college, they have a way to find out if you get it: the final exam. But what do consumers do? Rather than risk looking stupid, they

---

[34] http://www.lifehappens.org/reallifestories/.

tell you they need to think about it. They stop returning your calls. What seemed like a great interview because the prospect was shaking her head in agreement has gone bad. *People do not like ambiguity.* When people can't figure things out, it produces a fear response, and people who are fearful do not take action.

Your job is to present the solution in clear, concise terms. Make it easy to understand. When faced with complex decisions, we look for simple ways to decide. Too many options with too much information will result in choice overload. And remember, speak in terms of what the product does, not how it works. People are not looking for a simple product; rather, they want a simple way to decide. You need to judge carefully the amount of information a client can handle. Err on the side of less, and you will get more — sales, that is.

The following is a quote from a prospect in one of the focus groups used in the LIMRA study: "I started to tune out. I started to sit there in a state of confusion. 'What are you talking about?' With all the figures being thrown around, it was like, 'What am I buying, or what are you trying to sell?'" Prospects have a need to understand.

Confusion is viewed as a deception tactic. The more a person believes he or she is being double-talked, the less he or she will trust you. If your product is as good as you say it is, then why can't I understand what you are saying? A good exercise for you is to ask a close friend, a spouse, or a parent to sit through your presentation. When it's over, ask them to explain what you just told them. The results may surprise you.

3. Use heuristics.

The word "heuristic" comes from the Greek phrase "to find or discover." It involves experienced-based techniques that help in problem solving, learning, and discovery. A heuristic is a rule of thumb, an educated guess, an intuitive judgment, or, simply, common sense. Common sense rules of thumb not only help people make decisions, they also help people feel good about their decisions. Heuristics give people an idea about what others have done when dealing with the same subject. And we know people like to know that others have made the same decisions.

As a financial rep, you should be familiar with and ready to use rules of thumb with your prospects. For example, when someone asks you how much money he should save, you might say, "Many experts feel that, in addition to maxing out your retirement plans such as a 401(k) or IRA, you should save at least 10 percent of your take-home pay for other goals such as college, an emergency fund, or a new home. That is, if you start young. If you are over 40 and just starting to save, you may need 30 percent or more." And if he asks, "How much house should I buy?" your answer might be as follows: "If you are buying a home and don't want to feel stretched over hot coals for years to come, the home shouldn't cost more than two and a half times your gross income."

A prospect also might ask, "How much should I have when I retire?" You could answer like this: "Many experts suggest you have 20 times the amount of expenses you will have that won't be covered by pension or Social Security payments. The other rule of thumb is to assume you will need 70 percent to 100 percent of your income every year in retirement, given rising medical costs and longer, more active lifestyles in retirement."

> Common sense rules of thumb not only help people make decisions, they also help people feel good about their decisions.

Here's another typical question prospects and clients ask: "How much life insurance should I own?" Your answer, using rules of thumb, could be something like this: "If you are married with young children or teenagers, you will need a policy that covers between eight and 10 times your family income and possibly more, depending on family expenses and how much your surviving spouse can earn."

Some reps ask clients to go to the LIFE Foundation's website and use the life insurance calculator to see how much they should own. It is a great idea to use third-party rules of thumb. To establish the benefit the government paid to families of 9/11 victims, the Department of Justice used their own rule of thumb — up to 20 times each victim's income.

There is a lot of conventional wisdom around financial matters, and you should be able to use it to reassure your clients that they are doing the right thing and are not alone in this thinking.

4. Consider present value.

This is an interesting tactic because, contrary to what financial analysts and economists say, the general public does not consider present value as important when making decisions. *Current income flow is more important in their budgeting decisions than the present value of lifetime wealth.* Current income means consumers make decisions in terms of monthly budgets. You need to talk to them in terms of how your solution will help in many ways and how it will fit into their monthly budget. It can't be seen as an extra, and while in the first year they may have to squeeze it in, it must have a place and a purpose in their long-term budget.

5. Exhibit fairness.

This is about how you treat your prospects in the sales presentation. Do you get them involved? Do you listen to them? Do you respect the questions they ask? Always be sure that when prospects ask a question, you write it down on a piece of paper in front of them — especially if you want to wait to answer it later in your presentation. Failure to write it down could create suspicion on the part of prospects. They may sit there thinking you are not going to answer their question because the true answer is bad. If you can show them that they are being treated fairly, they are much more likely to trust your proposal.

6. Use visualization.

This is extremely important. How often to you find yourself buried in numbers? Paint *word pictures.* Help prospects see how ownership of the product and taking your advice will make them feel. Say things like, "Imagine how good it will feel to have those future grandkids of yours coming up to the lake house every weekend in the summer. Do you think you will teach them to fish, the same way your grandfather taught you?" Compare the difference between that and this: "At age 65, you will have accumulated $250,000 for your use." Self-enjoyment is a powerful feeling. Getting a sense of how something will make us feel even before we own it is what advertising agencies try to do to us all the time. "Virtual ownership" is a powerful tool in the sales process. Help prospects visualize the benefits they could receive by creating a compelling story about their financial goals.

7. Establish mental accounts.

People have a need to classify things they have and budget for into separate accounts. Whether they do this on paper or in their mind, it feels better when something fits into one of those boxes. And if the product you are recommending fits in more than one spot, all the better. This is why it's important to explain how a product like life insurance can fit into more than one account.

> People have a need to classify things they have and budget for into separate accounts. And if the product you are recommending fits in more than one spot, all the better.

Say to a prospect something like, "Mrs. Prospect, life insurance can help in many ways; first, of course, by providing an important benefit to your family if you should die prematurely. But assuming you don't die before age 65, which is quite likely, the money isn't gone; it's in an account that you can make cash withdrawals from and spend on that exotic vacation you always wanted to take. Or perhaps even better, it can be converted into a monthly income for a retirement check that you cannot outlive."

Another way you can help a prospect establish a mental account is to ask her to take a dollar bill out of her pocket. Then say to her, "If I ask you to give me that dollar bill, and I put it in my pocket and leave, how much has it cost you?" She might answer "One dollar" or "One dollar and 50 cents, because I had to pay taxes on it before I put it in my own pocket." Now ask her to put the dollar back into one of her pockets, but not the same one she took it out of. Then ask how much that transaction cost her. She will probably say, "Nothing because I still have the dollar." You would say, "That's exactly right, and life insurance works in much the same way. The money is still yours; it's just in a different pocket, doing different things for you and your family."

Study these concepts, and use them to establish a stronger relationship with your prospects and clients.

Three Sources of Human Behavior

Because you are probably among the 20 percent of people who can sell, you will enjoy hearing how a quote from Plato, one of the great Greek philosophers, can help us examine the work we do in the financial security business.

Plato said, "Human behavior flows from three main sources: desire, emotion, and knowledge." Let's examine these three sources of human behavior, beginning with knowledge, in the context of the work we do.

Knowledge

He who stops getting better, ceases being good, is another way of referring to lifelong learning. The challenge today's rep has is being disciplined enough to continue his or her education. Between continuing education requirements, home office schools, and new products, where do you find the time to really increase your knowledge, not just simply keep up? There are plenty of ways to gain significant knowledge, but it takes a real commitment to do it. I've heard all the excuses: "I am behind on my goals, so I have to focus on work." Or, "I need to make money; I have bills to pay." But even the best of them are not good excuses for not improving your skills.

What can you do? Schedule that American College course you've been putting off. Have you completed your designations? Is there another you should be pursuing? There are online programs available as well. But you must commit, and you must show up. I could always tell the reps who would be long-term successes. They were the ones who knew education imparted confidence — and confidence builds courage. Most reps fail to ask for referrals to "big" people because they do not have confidence in their ability.

Plato also had this to say about education: "If a man neglects education, he walks lame to the end of his life."

Emotion

This is the second source of human behavior, according to Plato, and it means any strong feeling. I want to examine one emotion, anger, and its role in helping us accomplish more.

Australian author Mary Garden said, "A wonderful emotion to get things moving when one is stuck is anger. It was anger, more than anything else, that had set me off, roused me into productivity and creativity."

To use anger properly, you have to understand a few things about it. First, the difference between what we have and what we want produces anger. This anger can be either hostile or passive. Neither is good.

However, if we can channel anger into assertive behavior, it can be enormously helpful in helping us get what we want out of life.

To do this, you need to create a list of haves and wants. Then, channel your anger by creating a plan of action. Once you have a plan, break it down to the first and simplest thing you have to do to get things moving. Very often, for us, it's getting a better prospect or even simply making that next phone call. If you can master harnessing your anger into an assertive yet productive plan, you will grow your business like you never thought possible.

Desire

I have a desire to inspire. What is your desire? Napoleon Hill, the author of *Think and Grow Rich*, said, "Desire is the starting point of all achievement, not a hope, not a wish, but a keen pulsating desire which transcends everything."

Do you have that feeling? Are you focused on something important that will drive you every day? A burning desire to be better, provide better, and excel? Desire is what makes life so wonderful. It's about accomplishing a goal and achieving at a high level. It's about getting what you want out of life, not wallowing in the valley of mediocrity. You must build that feeling.

I reversed Plato's three sources of human behavior on purpose so that I could leave you with what I believe is the most important one: desire. If you can find that one thing that you will do whatever it takes to achieve, you will create the emotion necessary to achieve it by channeling anger, and then you will seek the knowledge to do it. Desire is the starting point of human behavior. Without it, you are destined to never work hard enough, get enough, or care enough. You will never create the priorities in your life that help you sacrifice to achieve or to delay gratification until the price has been paid.

Mario Andretti, one of the greatest race car drivers of all time, said, "Desire is the key to motivation, but it is determination and commitment to an unrelenting pursuit of your goal, a commitment to excellence, that will enable you to succeed."

So start today. Work on your anger-management plan and create a burning desire to succeed.

The Best Car Salesman Ever

I had a personal experience in 2008 that got me thinking about reps and their success. It was one of those events that comes out of nowhere and yet has a significant impact. I was shopping for a new car for Bea and encountered a great salesman. And while this individual was selling automobiles, not an intangible product, he had many of the traits and characteristics of a great salesperson in any occupation.

Although I have my own car fetish and enjoy making a deal, I do not appreciate the haggling that is usually associated with buying a car. I find it too much of a game and have frequently walked out on salesmen who play it. You know, the old "Let me see what my manager thinks of your offer." Back and forth, wasting my time.

After doing a lot of research on the Internet, I marched into the dealership, ready to make a deal. As I walked in, I noticed that no one was at the reception desk. I walked past it and a number of small offices. I saw signs that said "Master Salesman" and "Certified Salesperson," but these supposedly above-average salespeople were reading newspapers and magazines. So I just kept walking. I knew the manager's office was in the corner, and that's where I was headed. Might as well go straight to the top, so I don't have to play the game, right?

Just as I was approaching the office, I saw a salesman with his hands full of papers heading in the other direction. He saw me, and suddenly I became the most important person in the place. He introduced himself, offered me a bottle of water, and said he would be right back. Off he went to drop off the paperwork from a deal he just closed. I later found out that I bought the fourth car he had sold that day. That's a good day in the car business.

He started by taking a few facts. Who was the car for? What were we interested in? Any particular reason for choosing his brand? How many miles would we drive it? What had we driven in the past? He asked a lot of questions before we headed out to see what I was interested in. This guy was fun! Big smile, firm handshake, easy to talk to, and well-dressed, too. You could tell that he took pride in his work. He was quick to tell me he was the leading salesperson three years running, but added that 2008 was a terrible year. "Thank God my old clients remembered me and came in and bought a few cars," he said. He mentioned that he had been at the dealership for 13 years after leaving a different job, adding that he had always wanted to sell cars. I believe he meant it.

After a few minutes of chit-chat, we went to look at the vehicle we were interested in. By that time, he was bubbling over with enthusiasm. I felt pretty smart because I obviously picked the greatest car ever built in the coolest color ever painted, steel gray. He put Bea and me in the front seat but reached over to demonstrate features like voice activation. He loved it. He thought that was such a cool feature. "The navigation is the best ever," he said. "And the sound system is unbelievable." This guy really knew his stuff.

I was reminded that competency is one of the key factors in building trust. He was competent. I didn't know the things he knew, but he convinced me he knew them. He said, with a laugh, "That with a lesson taught by the dealership's 'delivery expert,' even I could do it."

Next, we took it for a ride. As we test-drove the car, he continued to tell me what a great choice I was making, how his other customers had felt about that model, why his dealership was the best place to buy, and on and on. He assured me that if I had any problem at all with the car, he wanted me to call him, and he would call the service department.

At this point, I told him that if I got my price, I would buy then and there. "OK," he said, "let me go to work for you!" I had never heard that approach before. He said there was some room in the price and that he would get me the best price possible. I believed him, and that was key. His smile, his attention to detail, his knowledge, and his attitude all appealed to me. I was going to be happy buying this car from him. The manager wasn't quite as willing to let the car go for the price I wanted to pay, so we did end up haggling a bit, but we got it done. And I felt great!

Delivery was two days later. My salesperson called to confirm the time I was coming in and made sure I had all the papers I might need. He had arranged for the delivery expert to be ready and available. In short, it was one of my best-ever car-buying experiences.

What kind of experience do your prospects get? Have you taken the time to analyze your clients' experience? What do you think they would say about you?

Here is a checklist of some factors to keep in mind. Rate yourself on these factors using a scale from 1 to 5, with 5 being the best or highest rating, and see how you measure up.

> Most people like doing business with people who are gracious, smiling, friendly, enthusiastic, energetic, competent, trustworthy, reliable, and honest. Take the time before your appointment to put on your game face.

- Are you fully engaged from the minute you meet your prospect?

- Are you always smiling?

- Is your handshake firm?

- Are you dressed for success?

- Do you let people know you love what you do?

- Do you convey enthusiasm?

- Do you seem confident?

- Do you drop comments to imply you will be or have been around for a long time?

- Do you use stories about how other clients have felt?

- Do you demonstrate competence?

- Do you talk about the experts on your team and how they may be helpful in the future as needs change?

- Do you talk about why your company is the best one to buy from?

- Do you explain how you work and how you will follow up and follow through?

- Do you make sure your client knows you will be in touch regularly and that you hope you will do business again?

Most people like doing business with people who are gracious, smiling, friendly, enthusiastic, energetic, competent, trustworthy, reliable, and honest. Take the time before your appointment to put on your game face. Leave your troubles behind. Everyone has enough of their own; they don't need yours. After your appointment, ask yourself if you would buy from you.

I would be happy to refer anyone to my car salesman. He was the best I have seen in his industry. His colleagues — the other master salespeople — know all about the Cubs and Sox games, but that won't help them achieve their goals. They know about Lady Gaga, but that won't help them send their kids to college. They know all about the war in Afghanistan, but that won't help them hire more staff. They will go home at night and tell their spouses they had a tough day at the office and how the economy is really killing the car business. Take a lesson from my salesman. Bring your A game. Remember, I was his fourth sale of the day.

Sell With a Sense of Mission

I pose this question to the 20 percent who can sell: Is selling simply a necessary evil, or is it the drive train of the world's economy? I recently got to thinking about how reps — particularly the newer ones — present themselves in selling situations. They often act like they are a problem instead of a solution. They sometimes feel like they are imposing on people instead of helping like a good neighbor. They leave a sale quickly, often without asking for a referral, hoping the client doesn't change her mind while they are there. The way you feel about yourself during the selling process will have an enormous impact on your results.

Nothing happens until something is sold. Everything we use must be sold, but no one likes to *be sold to.* Put aside the financial services business for a minute and consider your personal attitude toward selling in general.

It may seem hard to believe, but I actually don't like salespeople. I don't like it when I walk into Bloomingdale's and someone approaches me as I walk in. I don't like it when I walk into Best Buy and someone asks me how they can help me. What is wrong with me? These people only want to help, right? Wrong. What they want to do is what they have been told to do: help me buy a product.

Today the Internet helps us break down the things we buy into categories: those we need help purchasing and those we don't. In other words, if we know what we want, how it works, and what it costs, we don't need the help of a salesperson. Not that having the help of a qualified person wouldn't help, but we would really just like to get it done without that uncomfortable encounter with a salesperson.

As long as we know our product, we can buy it unassisted today. Even a major purchase like an automobile can be made on the Internet. Why? Because we know what we want, and we know what it costs. We know the manufacturer, and we know the warranty period and what that means to us. When was the last time you had to ask a salesman what was covered under a warranty?

Four years ago, my seven-year-old grandson, Alex, went online to Zappos.com and bought a pair of shoes for himself. He told his mother about it after the purchase. He told her he knew his size and color, so he didn't need any help. The only problem was when the package arrived; it had three pairs of shoes in it. Apparently he wasn't sure the transaction went through and clicked three times to be sure. His mom sent two pairs back. Even a seven-year-old doesn't need help buying when he knows what he wants.

The sale of products will continue to grow online as people look for ways to avoid being sold to. It seems this feeling is pretty universal. We want the help of a salesperson only when we feel we need input. Then we want it from someone who is knowledgeable and trustworthy.

Isn't it ironic how often salespeople really do have something to offer and how often the products they have to offer can really help us? Take the pharmaceutical industry, for example. Think of all the miracle drugs

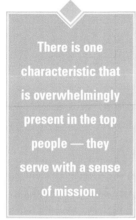

There is one characteristic that is overwhelmingly present in the top people — they serve with a sense of mission.

that pharmaceutical companies have created that contribute so much to our quality and length of life. Yet, in spite of that, the industry is often characterized as being all about attractive young salespeople pushing free samples at doctors' offices, where they are often considered a nuisance rather than a help. Every day, people are missing opportunities to improve their lives and make their work easier and more profitable because they don't want to talk to a salesperson.

So how do we, in the financial security business, work in an environment like this? As I have watched the industry for more than 40 years and met many successful representatives from many different companies, there is one characteristic that is overwhelmingly present in the top people — they serve with a sense of mission.

Successful selling is a mindset. It is not the words you use — many a silver-tongued wizard has failed. It is instead the rep's belief structure. The word "sell" derives from the Scandinavian root "selzig," which means to serve. (Hey, this is one word that isn't of Greek origin!) Those who become the elite selling stars of our industry have a service mindset.

Reps who believe they are serving others:

- Sell more

- Enjoy working more

- Never forget to prospect, because they want more people to serve

- Seek more education, so they can serve better

We sell products that help people solve problems. If we can promote, teach, and encourage the serving mindset, we will increase production and retention.

It was the great motivational speaker Zig Ziglar, who said, "You can get everything in life you want if you will just help *enough other people* get what they want." (I like to emphasize "enough" other people, so I added that.)

Don't let your prospects put you in that negative world of the pesky salesperson; always begin your day asking whom you can serve today. Use the words "I help people by ..."

The mission to serve can make such a difference in so many ways. As Norman Vincent Peale, the author of *The Power of Positive Thinking*, wrote: "The more you lose yourself in something bigger than yourself, the more energy you will have."

Losing sight of this core principle by focusing on a commission, a contest, or a big case will prevent you from ever being among the elite selling stars of our industry. Keep your eye on the real prize: the satisfaction you gain from helping others. That is the hallmark of an effective salesperson. If you have natural sales ability and you serve with a mission, you will rise to the top and achieve the Bountiful Life.

Stay in the Game

Another key to achieving continued success in sales is to have the tenacity to stay in the business after the novelty has worn off.

With each new year that approaches, you need to ask yourself this vital question: "What feels different about this coming year, compared to last year?" You must decide whether or not you want things to be different. Of course, it does depend on what stage you are at in the business. Are you at early-stage survival or mid-stage striving? Are you a late-stage new rep who is surging? Are you a senior who is still succeeding? Or are you in the period I call "predictable retrogression"? Al Granum called this "premature retrogression." I call it predictable retrogression because you can see it coming.

It begins as early as the fifth year and continues into the 20th-plus year of service. If, of course, you are like so many reps who begin their careers as interns or in their 20s, this is really dangerous. In that case, you need to think about your chronological age instead of years served. You need to stay in the game well into your 50s to avoid, as they often say in sports, peaking too early. The danger of peaking too early is boredom, lack of interest, no spark, no fun, and no recognition.

People who peak too early become chronic complainers and blamers. They never seem happy. They drop out of their ClientBuilder meetings and don't participate in contests. They avoid making commitments, and they stop learning. They miss meetings for any reason and always try to convince everyone that they are incredibly busy. They stop planning their futures and let outside influences control their lives.

A good friend of mine started to feel like he hit a plateau in his life. He was concerned that as a man in his early 50s he wasn't excited anymore. His courageous decision was to buy a new and bigger home. Yes, even as his children were growing up and heading to college, he was building a bigger home. He began to visualize his growing family: four children who would marry and have children. Grandkids who he and his wife would love. He was visualizing them all home for the holidays and staying in his big home.

I know this message is not popular with those of you on the precipice of retrogression, but give me a minute to help you fight this deadly fate.

In January 2012, the day after New Year's Day, I was watching a program that had a poll that asked how long people's resolutions would last. Remarkably, 36 percent reported that they had already broken their resolutions!

The best idea I know of for staying in the game is to create a five-year vision. Where do you see yourself in five years? What would you like to be doing? What kind of home do you want to be living in? What kind of car will you be driving? Where will you vacation? Where will your second home be? Do you have a bucket list for this five-year period?

After asking yourself these questions, ask how you will accomplish all of it, and set out to make it happen. Having a five-year plan to follow will keep you in the game. While you're at it, why not give back by teaming up with a young rep and sharing your wisdom? Participate in the MDRT mentoring program. Results show that mentors' production increases by an average of 18 percent while participating in the program. Team up with a young rep and make a run for it.

Stay in the game, and teach someone else how to do so. You will achieve the Bountiful Life while helping someone else achieve it, too!

Are You a Multiplier or a Divider?

Over the years, I have helped many reps do their goal setting, and it is always an interesting exercise. There are many things that go into the planning process. Things like self-worth — how much do you feel you are worth for what you do? Then there is the laziness factor. How willing are you to set up your environment to guard against letting it take over? Then there is your ability to "picture in your mind's eye" the things that are most important to you. Once you have your vision of the Bountiful Life, you can start putting the process in motion.

Put simply, reps fall into one of two broad categories: They are either Multipliers or Dividers.

Let's start with the Divider. The Divider is a rep who is just trying to get by. He or she focuses on minimums, likes to pace him or herself, and just gets by. This is the rep who has a really large case, let's say a $30,000 premium case. The rep's goal is to do $10,000 per month, and he says to himself, "I'm all set for three months."

Dividers
$30,000 divided by 3 = $10,000

Multipliers
$30,000 multiplied by 3 = $90,000

Then you have the rep who sees a bigger opportunity, the sky is the limit. This rep is a Multiplier. The Multiplier is the one who stretched him or herself thin to test the limits. Using the same example above, the Multiplier says, "If I can write one $30,000 premium case, I can do it again." What if I can do it four times in a year? What if I can do it once a month? And with this kind of thinking the rep begins to ask questions like, "Where did I get the prospect? What kind of income did he have? What illustration did I use? How can I find more just like this one?" Then that action goes into the plan.

So instead of doing $10,000 per month, for a total of $120,000, the rep finds four cases of $30,000 and has eight months of $10,000 and does $200,000 of premium for the year. You can make a huge difference in production by simply thinking like a Multiplier. Add to that the fact that Dividers usually come up short, and instead of writing $120,000 of premium, they finish the year about 10 percent short. Trust me. It happens all the time.

If you are really interested in the Bountiful Life you must think like a Multiplier!

Aiming for Success

Over the years, I have identified these three stages of success that seem to parallel the growth and development of a financial rep.

1. **The first stage of success involves working half-days — and you get to choose which 12 hours you will work!**

   Most new advisors are in this stage. But are you really working 12 hours, or are you just showing up? This includes WORK-ing to develop yourself during your driving time. We need 12 real hours of work per day to build this business, no less. You read day after day about the millions of people who have lost their jobs. So many people have been out of work for months — years, in many cases. Is there a reason you would jeopardize your career and face the possibility of joining the ranks of the 15 million Americans who are unemployed? Why do that? Choose to put in those few extra hours each day so you won't have to live without the things you desire.

   When I was growing up, I knew people who worked two or three jobs so that they could afford the things they wanted — schoolteachers who worked in grocery stores part time to make a little extra money, factory workers who put in overtime for the same reason. When I came into this business, I thought how great it was that my "extra job" could be the same as my "regular job." I could work nights doing the same job I did during the day.

   Too many people spend as little time as possible working, whether or not they have achieved a level of income to justify it. The more you learn about the business — the more time you put in — the easier things become over time, but you must pay the price.

   A speaker I heard at a meeting years ago said, "Everyone wants to know how to make $100,000 a year, but then they ask a person making $20,000 how to do it."

"You will never do anything in this world without courage. It is the greatest quality of mind next to honor."

—Aristotle

Are you a job-taker or a job-maker? Job-takers show up in the morning, and they have a full inbox. Their job is to move everything from their inbox to their outbox in the allotted time. Job-makers, on the other hand, are the people who put all the work in the job-takers' inboxes. This is the job of the successful rep — making things happen.

2. **The second stage of success comes a while later, when you can put a sign in your store window that says, "Open 24 Hours."**

When a customer comes by and you're not there, you can tell them, "I'm available 24 hours a week, not 24 hours a day." That's some distance down the road for most, but there is certainly a fair share of reps who have earned the right to say just that. It comes with earned success.

To achieve this level of success requires that you either get more "at-bats" or achieve a higher batting average. A combination of both is ideal.

A few years back, MDRT conducted a study about its members and discovered that the average member, who does about $200,000 of premium per year, works 58 hours per week.[35] Do you?

The average Court of the Table member does three times the base, or $600,000 of premium, and works 54 hours per week. Do you?

The average Top of the Table rep produces six times the base and works 51 hours per week. These producers make a ton of money. Do you?

Albert Einstein defined insanity as "doing the same thing over and over again and expecting different results." The recession may have helped define a new meaning of insanity: doing the same thing over and over again and expecting the *same* result.

We have always said that keeping 60 face-to-face appointments is *the job*, not a great job. Many advisors try to skate by on 40 to 50 kept appointments per month or less. I doubt this level of effort is getting them the results they desire.

---

[35] http://gamaweb.com/wp-content/uploads/2012/10/2011ResourceDirectory.pdf. p.4.

An associate once asked me why in the dead of winter, when no one is out golfing, our offices were empty on Fridays. He remarked that "you could shoot a cannon through the building and not hurt a soul." Remember: Smart, dedicated reps are willing to pay the price for success in advance.

This is the stage of development where you have learned to excel. Doing the same old stuff won't get you here, so it is up to you to fix it or change it. Practice management is the name of the game. Think about the one thing you could change immediately to make a real difference in your practice. Then do it!

3. **In the third stage of success — the one every person dreams about — you are so successful that you can put a sign in your store window that reads, "Gone fishing. Be back when I am done!"**

That is my favorite. That is the sign my good friend Brud Hodgkins' father put in the window of his grocery store years ago. To me, that is a person who has worked hard in the past and now has the wherewithal to do it his way. This is a time to cherish, once earned. There is convincing evidence that you can get there, but it will require that you think about your business differently than you have in the past. This is the Bountiful Life.

If you are to have the kind of breakthroughs you need to be successful in this business, you must go through a cycle of success. New reps must complete two stages of development:

▪ **Stage One.** The first step in stage one is to find prospects. As a new rep, nothing is more important right out of the gate than prospecting. Without good prospects in sufficient numbers, you will surely fail. That first day we send reps out to prospect is painful. They are scared. They don't know if they can do it, and they need to be field-tested. Once they get a few prospects under their belts, then the most important thing becomes making a commission. If they don't get some sales pretty quickly, they will have to leave the company, whether they want to or not. And they are acutely aware of this fact.

After they know they can generate a commission, then making a good sale becomes what they think about. Finally, they have the satisfaction of knowing they helped someone in a significant way coupled with the validation that comes with that knowledge.

That's a great place to be, right? Wrong!

That is when the business, which was so dreadfully hard to get started in, becomes boring — at least that's what I have heard from a number of good reps over the years. That's why I decided long ago that my job was "to create an environment in which reps can grow and continue to grow personally, professionally, and financially." Bored people don't grow: They go — elsewhere. In other words, they physically leave or emotionally quit.

Stage Two. In this stage the formula repeats itself, but it takes you and your practice to a higher level. Once again, the most important element is the prospect, but this time it's not just any prospect; it's a better, more challenging, harder-to-reach prospect. One who gets your eyes open wide and your adrenaline flowing. One who gives you butterflies in your stomach. You might have trouble sleeping the night before the appointment.

Not your usual prospect. This prospect is where growth comes from. This is where you get a challenge, as well as recognition that you just got better. It's a personal best.

With these types of opportunities, you are not growing simply because you grunted out 10 percent more premium this year than last year. You grow because you harness your talents and really figure this business out. You find a better, more efficient way of making big things happen. You emerge out of your comfort zone and move onto a bigger stage. This is about education, staff, methods, and mostly the courage to grow!

Once you have the super prospects, you focus not on the commission but on the sale and the tremendous feeling that comes with the quantum leap. It's the step that takes you to a higher place. So prospect to the highest level you can. Reach for the stars. You aren't likely to win mega millions on a scratch-off ticket, but you *can* when you succeed in this business!

ClientBuilders: Committing to Accountability

In their quest for success, many executives and sales reps spend thousands of dollars to join YPO (Young Presidents' Organization), a worldwide network for business leaders, or TEC, a professional-development group for CEOs, presidents, and business owners. They join these organizations to obtain accountability, ideas, and feedback.

In our business, we have ClientBuilder meetings to enhance productivity and foster success. If we are to succeed at a high level, we must set up our environment to promote success. A commitment to a ClientBuilder is one of the systems for success that does just that.

The first pillar of a ClientBuilder is accountability, which is enhanced by recordkeeping and reporting. Some business owners keep records, some don't. Some use goals to improve, some don't. Some report numbers, some don't. And some who want to report their progress have no one to report it to. So keep records. Set goals. Report numbers. Report progress.

Our system is superior because if we are dedicated, we can report numbers to a group of peers who understand our business and who are ready to help. We know that measurement improves performance. Anything we can measure, we can improve.

Those who join a ClientBuilder group must make three commitments:

- **A commitment to the group.** This commitment requires that you show up, even when you haven't had a good month. American writer Sam Ewing said, "Hard work spotlights the character of people. Some turn up their sleeves, some turn up their noses, and some don't turn up at all." When I was moderating a ClientBuilder group and a member was absent without notifying me, the first thing I would do was look at his or her production report. In about 90 percent of all cases, the absent rep had had a poor month. Hiding is not fulfilling a commitment to the group. You must come to ClientBuilder all the time, not just in the good months. Your commitment to the group is that you will always be there to give feedback to those who need it. It's not just about you.

  Failing to show up is not an option if you commit to your group. The group gels only when members know they can count on one another. This must become a priority, not an obligation. You are reporting to a group of interested people, not just the facilitator. Some want to help you learn more, and some want to learn from you. There is no room for selfish behavior.

- **A commitment to the business.** A great ClientBuilder is composed of people who are committed to the business through their dedication to high activity, lifelong learning, and goal setting. These three elements are essential in a strong group. Coming to ClientBuilder meetings to report good numbers keeps other distractions from taking over your precious hours each day.

■ **A commitment to yourself.** Being open to learning helps you improve your skills and is also a key to successful ClientBuilders. Epictetus said, "It is impossible for a man to learn what he thinks he already knows." Our business is about learning, and when you commit to learning, you will never be bored in your work. The difference between those who are students of the business and those who simply repeat a learned skill can be measured in thousands of dollars.

Managers' guidance is critical when you are new in the career and building the base for your growth. My good friend, Dennis Tamcsin, who appointed me general agent in 1977, used to say, "Financial reps become what they learn in the beginning." But reliance on this guidance over a long period of time demonstrates a lack of personal responsibility. I like to say, "Good managers are like good parents: They become progressively unnecessary." They're essential in the beginning, and the kids learn to walk, and then run. Then you send the kids to school and finally to college. Then, hopefully, you have a productive human being, capable of standing on his or her own, who can become your best friend. That is what makes me the happiest, when reps accept responsibility for themselves, mature, and own their success.

Your commitment to yourself must include a commitment to continual improvement. Nothing is more important. After 35 years as a successful managing partner, you wouldn't think I would need to attend four study group meetings per year plus a national meeting for managers, which I have attended for 32 consecutive years without a miss. But I do. I walk my talk to help you walk yours. Bill Gates said, "Success is a lousy teacher. It seduces smart people into thinking they can't lose." Don't ever be seduced into thinking you can't lose. You must keep learning.

> "Our words reveal our thoughts; our manners mirror our self-esteem; our actions reflect our character; our habits predict our future."
>
> —William Arthur Ward

Inspiration writer William Arthur Ward said, "Our words reveal our thoughts; our manners mirror our self-esteem; our actions reflect our character; our habits predict our future."

Make a habit of attending ClientBuilder meetings. It's one of the ways you can set up your environment to ensure success.

Achieving Success by Mastering Self-Talk

A man walks into a huge bookstore, wanders around a few minutes, and finally says to the clerk, "Can you tell me where the self-help section is?"

The clerk replies, "If I told you, that would defeat the purpose, wouldn't it?"

While that's kind of funny, self-help is not. Think about the thousands of things we think about every day, all the conversations we have in our mind. I often feel like I have two guys sitting on my shoulders, one on each side. One is pulling me one way, and the other is pulling me the opposite way. This battle goes on for all of us. Mastery of the conversations we have with ourselves is one of the keys to success. Learning how to manage your thinking is extremely important.

Think about all the things we do on any given day — things that are good for us and things that are not. Temptations abound. You go to your favorite coffee shop, and there are the pastries. You get to the office, and there are your colleagues ready to talk about sports. You decide to work on the big case proposal instead of dialing for appointments. Choices, choices, and *more* choices.

You become what you think about. Paul J. Meyer, a self-help guru, said it best in this quote that I have repeated in one form or another for 40 years: "Whatever you vividly imagine, ardently desire, sincerely believe, and enthusiastically act upon must inevitably come to pass." This is so important. We have to transform dreams into goals, and we can do that only by mastering our self-talk.

My good friend and managing partner in Orlando, Florida, Joe Meier, once sent a message to his reps that illustrates what I am getting at here. It is an important case of "mind over what matters." Joe's message to his reps was a quote from self-help author and success coach Anthony Robbins: "The way we communicate with others and with ourselves ultimately determines the quality of our lives."

I am sure you have heard that the single biggest factor in success is the ability to communicate effectively. It has been proven, over and over, that looks and intelligence do not determine your level of success; your ability to communicate effectively does. I really like that Robbins' quote because it addresses not only your outgoing communication with others but also your self-talk — your constant communication with yourself. In fact, I would say that the best outward communicators are also the best inward communicators. Their positive self-talk lays the groundwork for what they ultimately communicate to others.

Do you believe that the way we communicate with others and with ourselves ultimately determines the quality of our lives? I have a test for you. On a scale from 1 to 10 (with 10 being the best), how would you rate how well you communicate with others? Using the same scale, how would you rate how well you communicate with yourself?

My guess is that the two scores are very close to each other or the same. If they are far apart, I would examine why that is and ask what you can do about it. Assuming they are close or the same, what can you do to improve your scores? My recommendation is to start improving your self-talk. If you can change your inward communication, then most certainly your outgoing communication will change too.

I want to describe what I have learned about positive self-talk from all the tapes, CDs, books, and speakers whose messages I have spent time absorbing during the past four decades. These are three positive phrases that I have repeated to myself literally hundreds of times and that have had a positive impact on me:

- **"If you believe, you are believed."** If you believe you are there to help other people, that your service to others is worthwhile and important, that your company is the best, that your client's life will be more fulfilled as a result of working with you, and that by helping others get what they want, you will get everything you want, then it will be so. That mindset has helped me deal with the procrastination and rejection that is part of what we do. Believing in what I am doing and how I am doing it is very empowering.

"I can handle this." This is perhaps the most important thing I say to myself. It doesn't matter how dramatic, hurtful, critical, or painful a situation is, if I tell myself "I can handle this," I will find a way to do just that. Having a positive attitude that it will be OK, even if it is not all right at the time, has been critical to much of what I have accomplished

> Start improving your self-talk. If you can change your inward communication, then most certainly your outgoing communication will change too.

in my life. Let me assure you, I could swap war stories with just about anyone about the challenges I have had to address in my life. We all have and will face great challenges in our lives in the coming years. I see people either handle them well or become mentally paralyzed by circumstances beyond their control. Instead of doing the best they can under the circumstances, they stop doing productive things in their life and focus only on the matter at hand. Don't do that. Tell yourself, *I can handle this*, and you will find a way to do so.

"If it is to be, it is up to me." This is an absolute truth. Although our world and career are full of abundance, you must make your own breaks. It is there for the taking, but we each must do the taking. Disciplining yourself to do the right things when they are supposed to be done will ultimately get you where you want to be. Every day you are confronted with countless choices, so get in the habit of making the right ones for you. Winning that daily battle is up to you, but each day you do, success will be your companion.

Effective communication is paramount to your life, my life, and everyone else's life. Focus on how you are communicating with others and yourself, and then improve on it. By doing so, you will reach levels of success you have heretofore only dreamed of. There is much more for you out there. Go get it!

We can spend millions of dollars on training, thousands of dollars on fancy clothes, and hundreds of dollars on lunches, and none of it will pay off until you master "mind over what matters." What matters is what you want out of life, what is really important to you. What matters is your family. What matters is your children's education. What matters is your community. Don't settle for mediocrity.

All of the successful people I know have taken control of this part of their lives. It may take some practice, but you can do it, too. And it all begins with positive self-talk.

Think Like a Rookie

My friend Jon Gordon once said, "I know I'm getting older when I step on a regional jet and the pilot looks like he just graduated from high school. Truth is, I want a pilot with experience, not someone who learned to fly on a PlayStation."

> Rookies create their good old days right now. Rookies put their heads down, work hard, stay positive, live fearlessly, and are naïve enough to be successful.

I desire a pilot with experience, too, but it occurred to me that experience is not always a good thing.

In fact, sometimes experience can be a curse, such as when your experience in business causes you to focus on the good old days, when everyone was making money, when everyone was successful, when life was easier, and when you didn't have to go after business because it came to you.

I've noticed that in a challenging economy, a lot of people are inflicted with the curse of experience. They complain about the way things are, long for the way things were, and dream about what could have been — if only the economy hadn't crashed. The good news is that there is a simple antidote to the curse of experience, and that is to think like a rookie.

Rookies don't have experience, and they don't know how things were. They have no knowledge of the good old days. Instead, rookies create their good old days right now. Rookies put their heads down, work hard, stay positive, live fearlessly, and are naïve enough to be successful.

I recently spoke at a national sales meeting for a Fortune 500 company. While the president was speaking, he recognized a rookie salesperson from the stage for winning a big account, saying, "He didn't know that what he asked for to win the account doesn't usually happen. He didn't know that you don't just ask for it. If he were a veteran, he would have just assumed the answer would be no. But he did ask, and the answer was 'yes.'"

Rookies aren't tainted by rejection, negative assumptions, or past experiences. Rookies don't focus on what everyone says is impossible. Instead, they believe anything is possible. They bring an idealism, optimism, and passion to their work, and because they believe in the future, they take the necessary actions to create it.

So, regardless of how much experience you have in this industry and your profession, I want to encourage you to let your experience be a blessing, not a curse. Let your experience provide you with expertise, and let your rookie mindset fuel you with optimism and passion.

If you're an industry veteran, mentor the rookies, because for all their effort and energy, they do make mistakes. And let them teach you how to see the world through their eyes.

Some reps never play like rookies. They are afraid to get in the game. Veteran reps would have a lot more fun if they would establish just a bit of reckless abandon in their practices. So have some fun, get in the game, and make some plays. If you try it, it just might change your life. Think like a rookie, forget the past, and create your good ol' days right now. That's how you earn success.

Live Our Core Values: Passion, Growth, Personal Responsibility

I recently read the book *Mastering the Rockefeller Habits: What You Must Do to Increase the Value of Your Growing Firm* by Verne Harnish. His discussion of core values got me thinking that perhaps I should articulate our core values more often, so I shall.

The mission of the Hoopis Financial Group was to "create an environment in which financial representatives can grow, and continue to grow, personally, professionally and financially." This was our mission for more than 30 years. When I talk about this, I always say that the most important part of the statement is to help reps continue to grow.

Although learning the basics of our business and getting started as a new rep is difficult, once you get your footing, it becomes much easier. However, this ease can become somewhat boring if you are not challenged to grow further. I have always made it a high priority to help reps grow. It would be easy to say, "Let them figure it out for themselves," but that wouldn't be right. It was my personal commitment to help my firm's reps continue to grow.

Closely tied to our mission statement were our three core values: passion, growth, and personal responsibility. Let's examine each in some detail.

- **Passion.** This is where it all begins — having a passion for what we do. Remember, first you get in the financial security business, then it gets in you. What that really means is that until you experience the benefits you bring to the people you work with, you cannot fully experience the enormity of the impact you have on people. Until new reps have their own stories, they have to borrow some from veteran reps to help prospects grasp the impact reps have. What we do is so important. We are on a mission, with a passion to help people save more money, plan for retirement, and of course be sure their plan is complete whether they live too long, die too soon, or become disabled. We make sure children who unfortunately lose a parent get to stay in their home, get a great education, and have a parent waiting for them when they get home after school. Doctors save lives; we save lifestyles!

  No one can do this in a stroke of a pen but us. At a 2010 LIMRA meeting, a speaker made this compelling statement: "Parents worry a lot about bathing their kids in hand sanitizer so they won't get sick, while one of nine parents won't live to see their children graduate from college." We need to help parents realize the importance of owning adequate amounts of life insurance in case they don't make it. That's where our passion needs to be.

- **Growth.** When I talk about growth as a core value, I am talking about a commitment each and every person in this business must make to get better at what we do. You must make a commitment to growth through lifelong learning. You must pursue the professional designations of our industry. You should consider CLU and ChFC to be the least you will achieve, not the goal. He who stops getting better ceases being good. And when we see the compelling evidence that those with designations make nearly twice as much as those without them, the decision becomes obvious. You owe it to yourself, your family, and your clients to be the very best you can be.

- **Personal responsibility.** This is what drives your success. It is not what we can supervise, it's not checking numbers, and it is not taking attendance. It is your personal commitment to doing the right things. To show up when you sign up. To manage your business in a way that proves, beyond any doubt, that you are committed to success, no matter what it takes. Personal responsibility is where the rubber meets the road. You will never achieve your potential without it. This is not a dress rehearsal; we are really living life every day to be the best we can be. Don't come up short.

Living the core values of your organization opens the door to getting what you want out of life for you and your family. If you are living some of those values but not all, decide now to build the rest of the core values into your plan. Take time to assess your practice, and ensure you are in the game to win.

Realize That Harsh Words or Actions Last Forever

There once was a little girl who had a bad temper. Her mother gave her a bag of nails and told her that every time she lost her temper, she must hammer a nail into the back of the fence.

The first day, the girl drove 37 nails into the fence. Over the next few weeks, as she learned to control her anger, the number of nails she hammered daily gradually dwindled. She discovered it was easier to hold her temper than to drive those nails into the fence.

Finally, the day came when the girl didn't lose her temper at all. She told her mother about it, and the mother suggested that the girl now pull out one nail for each day she was able to hold her temper. The days passed, and the young girl was finally able to tell her mother that all the nails were gone.

The mother took her daughter by the hand and led her to the fence. She said, "You have done well, my daughter, but look at the holes in the fence. The fence will never be the same. When you say things in anger, they leave a scar just like this one."

Have you ever been in a state of rage and, in an attempt to make yourself feel better, told someone off? How did it feel right at that moment? Thirty minutes later? The next day? Probably not as good as you were hoping. Your next thought was that maybe you went too far, said too much, or hurt someone. So you decide to apologize, and when you do, the victim of your rage is gracious, smiles, and tells you not to worry about it. It's water over the dam, water under the bridge. Or is it?

Unfortunately, most of the time it is a ruined relationship, forever changed. Have you ever done this with an underwriter? Those poor people. They must go through special training to be able to take what some of you dish out from time to time. But then you send popcorn, flowers, or candy and expect everything to be all right. How about with friends or your spouse? These are difficult situations, to say the least. Just remember, *when you lose your temper, the victim usually ends up the victor.* You give up your power when you become angry. Successful people don't let their anger get the best of them. They handle difficult situations with aplomb.

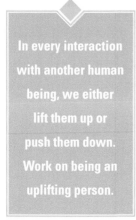

In every interaction with another human being, we either lift them up or push them down. Work on being an uplifting person.

I was once given this advice: "Never tell a person to go to hell, for two reasons. First, they won't go there. Second, they will never forget you told them to go there." It's tough for people to trust someone who has hurt them. It is indeed hard to look at a person who has told you to go to Hades and not remember that moment. It's similar to remembering where you were when President Kennedy got shot or when the space shuttle blew up or when 9/11 happened. These events leave an indelible mark on our memory.

So the moral of the story: Don't let your actions or words leave scars behind. How? While I can't tell you what not to do, I can tell you what *to* do. If your actions or words result in someone saying "thank you" or "I appreciate that," you are on the right track. When your actions or words bring a smile to someone else's face, you are on the right track.

We are in a relationship-*building* business. You need to think about what you do, how you look, and what you say. There are no days off from good behavior. In every interaction with another human being, we either lift them up or push them down. Work on being an uplifting person.

See how many times people tell you "thank you" or "I appreciate that" in a day or a week. The amazing thing is that we can dramatically impact our positive responses through our actions and words, the same way the girl pounded a nail into the fence when she got angry and pulled one out when she held her temper. You can make the same type of decision about your actions and words. When you do, just like the girl, you will be changed forever. We all have room to improve, even if we are better than most. So go for it!

Why We Shouldn't Compare Ourselves to Others

About our school work, my father used to tell my brothers and me, "I expect all A's or under on your report card, but I expect a 10 for effort." We often laughed at that comment until we realized how serious he was about achieving a 10 on a 10-point scale for effort. Looking back, his brilliance in this area has been confirmed over and over in my life. To paraphrase management guru Peter Drucker, develop your strengths, and you can render your weaknesses irrelevant. Successful people develop their strengths and manage their weaknesses, and they never compare themselves to other people.

It's hard to imagine a lot of the time, but the people you admire got it wrong before they got it right. They may make success look easy, but you don't know what they've been through to get there. The Bible says, "But when they measure themselves by one another and compare themselves with one another, they are without understanding" (2 Corinthians 10:12).[36] We are all given different talents, and they determine our potential.

I have always advised reps not to compare themselves to others, despite the fact that it is a very natural and tempting thing for us to do in a production-oriented business like ours. And while our agency did foster this tendency through contests, bulletins, and recognition, in personal planning, it's important to look only at yourself. Look at your own targets, goals, and objectives only, no one else's.

If instead of looking at your own targets you look to the right, you might see a rep doing less than you are, and this could give you a false sense of success. You might even take your foot off the pedal. Measure yourself against *your* goals and your God-given talent. And if you look to the left and there is a rep doing better than you, it might be discouraging. You might give up, when in reality, you are doing very well compared to your goals and the level to which you have developed your talent at that point in time.

Like my father, I expect a 10 in effort. Where would you say you are on the 1-to-10 effort scale? Have you assessed your strengths and weaknesses?[37] Do you have a plan to develop your talents? Do you know how to manage your weaknesses? Have you hired an assistant who is good at the tasks you're not good at?

Over and over again, we are reminded that having a development plan is essential. We also are reminded that we are all blessed with different strengths, and we need to recognize them. If you are not clear about your strengths, talk to your mentor or spouse about them. Once you are clear about what they are, ask yourself, "On a scale of 1 to 10, with 10 being an all-out effort to be the best I can be, how am I doing?" Most of you will answer 6, 7, or 8. Not good enough. We all have the ability to work hard for 10 hours a day, to improve, and to stay focused. But you will improve only if it is important enough to you to achieve the Bountiful Life and have the time and money to enjoy life, family, and friends to the fullest.

Successful people do what is expected of them each day — plus a little bit more. (Remember, do extra ordinary things.) Strive for progress, not perfection.

---

[36] *New American Standard Bible.* http://www.biblegateway.com/passage/?search=2%20Corinthians%20 10:12&version=NASB.

[37] A variety of assessment tools are available at www.hoopis.com.

Have a Plan B

Successful people do what is expected of them each day — plus a little bit more. Strive for progress, not perfection.

A lot of business is written by accident, or chance, but you have to be out where the "accidents" are happening. I often wonder why some reps don't have a Plan B in place so that when a day blows out, you are ready to make things happen in spite of it. Remember, between 9:00 a.m. and 5:00 p.m. you should either be at an appointment or fighting like hell to make one.

It also concerns me when reps show up to the office dressed casually, as if to say, "Nothing good is going to happen today." I have professed for years that a rep can be extremely successful working 200 days per year. But those are working days. That leaves 30 additional days for training and meetings and 30 days for vacation and family time, not including weekends. But on those 200 days, you must be out where the "accidents" are.

Have a Plan B. It could be a place of business where you can go to bump into people or a particular client you can drop in on. Have a list of people you can stop in to see anytime. Anything is better than sitting in your office waiting for a call to come in.

Five Barriers to Success — Four Are Fatal

To establish a career in the financial services industry, there are five barriers to success you must overcome. Like any career, we know it takes time to establish mastery. In Malcolm Gladwell's book *Outliers*, he talks about the 10,000-hour rule, in which he explains that a person needs 10,000 hours of experience to gain mastery of a skill. Over the time it takes to invest 10,000 hours in your pursuit, you will confront many hurdles you must overcome to realize the Bountiful Life. Knowing what those hurdles are is critical to your ability to navigate them. Think about hurdlers in track and field. Hurdlers know from practice how many steps they have between each hurdle. This allows them to keep a stride as they race. The time it takes to finish the race and making it over the hurdle are what determines the winner, not how well he or she jumped the hurdle. There are no points for style. For us, reaching the Bountiful Life is how we determine the winner, not how we looked getting there. You don't have to look good as you take on these barriers; you just have to do whatever it takes to overcome them.

Here are the five barriers to success in our business, posed as questions:

1. Can you sell?

Most of you reading have probably already crossed the first barrier. If you are reading this, you most likely know that you are among that 20 percent of people on the planet who can sell, at least to friends and family. This phase of your career takes only two or three months to determine. Reps who discover they cannot sell typically leave the business after that amount of time. Management works hard to avoid recruiting this type of person because they use up a lot of valuable time.

2. Can you sell to strangers?

This second barrier is obviously very important because you cannot keep growing in the business if you don't develop the relationship-building skills that allow you to connect with and earn the trust of your prospects. The questions you must answer here include:

- Can you break out into the big world?

- Can you go beyond your natural market (friends and relatives)?

- Are you able to leverage your relationships with your friends and relatives to meet the hundreds of people they know?

- Do they trust you enough to give you those names?

- Do you have the confidence in yourself to continue to prospect and network?

It takes about six months to know if you can overcome this barrier, and you need to master prospecting techniques to do so. Managers and mentors must be sure reps are learning to prospect early on.

3. Can you survive becoming an expert?

Overcoming this barrier takes more time and effort than the first two. This is where you have to master the task of juggling CLU, ChFC, and CFP classes and tests while maintaining your production. This is also where a little knowledge is a dangerous thing, and you may develop the frequently fatal career disease described earlier: "big case-itis." Here is where reps trade a career for a case, losing focus and attention and allowing one case to consume all of their time. Most don't make it through this phase. It takes three to five years to make it, and only the best get through. This is where you really need to keep your eyes open and ask for help when you need it. Maintaining accountability, attending ClientBuilder groups, receiving mentoring, and meeting high expectations are mandatory in this phase. The good news is that if you can survive this phase, your chances of reaching the Bountiful Life have now turned in your favor.

4. Can you reach the highest levels of productivity?

If you cannot, don't panic. It is not fatal to your career. There are many reps who, while not doing all they are capable of, can still make a great living. The level of success you rise to is often determined by your ability to organize time and function, through self-discipline and delegation. You must learn to be efficient and effective, spending your time doing only the most important tasks and getting maximum face time in front of clients and prospects. This is where you realize you really are an expert, you are making a lot of money, and you are bringing true worth to society. This typically occurs after five years in the business.

5. Can you handle success?

This topic is the source of some of the world's most spectacular crashes! In this phase, you are organized, you are experienced, and you are an expert. You are grossing between $500,000 and $1 million a year. You are asked to do speaking engagements, you are called a success, and you are highly visible. But then it happens, and we have seen this a lot in the news, you become too good for your spouse, colleagues, friends, and even some clients. You're money-mad and outgrow your hat size. You pull away from the very people who have cheered you on for the past 10 years. You might drop out of your ClientBuilder group and avoid company meetings. You forget who brought you to the dance.

The first four barriers are tests of ability, talent, and hard work, while the fifth is a test of character. In this phase, failure is easier than success. If you fail, you can go back to the familiar territory of mediocrity. Success has taken you to new ground, and now you have to learn how to deal with it. I have always said, "If you give money to a good person, you make a better person; if you give money to a bad person, you make a worse person." You have to manage this one carefully. There is great potential here for both good and evil.

If you survive the fifth barrier, if you can handle success, you are indeed ready to enjoy the Bountiful Life and will have the time and money to enjoy your family and friends. You can reach this phase in as few as 10 years, which should be approximately 10,000 hours spent in face-to-face time with clients and prospects, and with that you will achieve mastery. This assumes you spend half of your time in front of prospects and clients during that 10-year period.

We know the barriers, and we can see the hurdles. There should not be any surprises. Take each barrier as it comes. Don't look ahead. Instead, focus on what you need to do to overcome the barrier in front of you. Trust me, it's worth it.

Setting Goals to Stay on Track

11

In 2008, I was invited to participate in an "exceptional leaders" coaching program under the direction of the world-renowned Robert K. Cooper, Ph.D. Dr. Cooper is a pioneer in the neuroscience of human capacity, leadership, trust, and initiative. An advisor to organizational leaders and an acclaimed educator on how exceptional leaders and teams excel under pressure while everyone else is just competing or falling behind, Dr. Cooper is also known for his work on the practical application of emotional intelligence in leadership and organizations.

"Dignity does not consist in possessing honors, but in deserving them."

—Aristotle

During that coaching program, I had many revelations about my life's work and how I would like to use my final four years as the managing partner of Hoopis Financial Group. My decision was to work to double the agency's premium production by the end of May 2012. For me to accomplish my objective, I had to help each and every one of my reps do the same.

In 2008, I handpicked a group of about 30 top advisors and began writing my blog, Hoopis Forum Focus, with them as my primary focus. Then I handed over new-rep development to an extremely capable team. My goal at the time was to double those reps' productivity and have them reach Forum production that year. The key was to increase those 30 top reps' production so others would follow their lead.

I also decided that we needed to set a new standard of performance. So in 2008, achieving MDRT status was no longer the goal: It became the minimum acceptable behavior a rep could exhibit for him or her to be a contributing member of the agency. The new objectives became Forum, (approximately two times MDRT), Court of the Table, and Top of the Table.

Many reps were just entering the peak earning years of their life and had at least 15 years left in which they could accumulate wealth and thus provide everything they have ever dreamed of for their families. But if you are to achieve greatness, you must continue to do the things that got you here in the first place: client building and high activity.

Remember what Albert Gray said about why people fail to achieve: "It is easier to accept the hardship of making a poor living than it is to accept the hardship of making a better one." If you are 35 to 50 years old, you are now in reach of the majority of the wealth in this country. Who better than you to collect some of it?

My favorite elevator speech, when someone asks what I do, is this: "I sell life insurance to wealthy people and have become so myself!" Why not? Why not you? Easy jobs don't pay much, and, unfortunately, the challenge of our business is getting started in it, but it becomes easy to stay in it, although sometimes in a mediocre way.

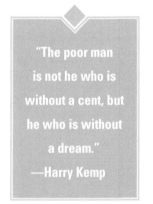

"The poor man is not he who is without a cent, but he who is without a dream."
—Harry Kemp

Work each day. Try to vividly and clearly envision your best work and life five years out. Then ask yourself, is the way I have planned my time and choices today the best way to make the future I envision a reality? If not, what can I do differently to make it happen now?

Harry Kemp, America's "vagabond poet," said, "The poor man is not he who is without a cent, but he who is without a dream."

Goal setting, mechanics, and achievement are tools you need to hold close if you are to succeed. The dream is the why, and the goal is the how. A dream without a goal is just a way to pass the time. A goal without a dream is a short-term objective without lifelong impact. A dream is a fantasy waiting to become a reality. This can happen only with an action plan that puts your heart and soul in the dream. It has been said that in the absence of clearly defined goals, we become strangely loyal to performing daily acts of trivia. As George Burns said, "Look to the future because that is where you'll spend the rest of your life."

Setting goals helped our agency achieve a level of success we would have thought impossible years earlier. Likewise, you must set goals to achieve the next level of success. Top performers set goals.

Understand Move-Toward and Move-Away Goals

As we set goals early on in our lives, we do what is needed to achieve them. How ambitious those goals are determines the effort required to meet them. We have all set achievable goals that, when reached, provided limited and shallow satisfaction. To gain more satisfaction, we need to set more substantial goals. With that comes more work, more reward, and more personal satisfaction and growth. It becomes a circle of success as those who choose to continually set meaningful goals set out to achieve them.

Goals are like stairs. We take one at a time and reach a new level with each step we take. Then we have a tendency to plateau. This plateau becomes our comfort zone, which doesn't really exist, because over time even what we consider comfortable becomes rather uncomfortable. The longer we stay in the comfort zone, the more difficult it becomes to generate the steam required to move to the next step. We get tired and satisfied and begin to have conversations with ourselves in which we decide we have enough. "Why do I need more? I don't want to spoil the kids. Why do we need to go away on vacation? Let's just enjoy being home for a change." And on and on. A better way to approach success is to reset the goal to the next step and move forward before your discipline muscle begins to atrophy. That's where the fun is.

I am reminded of the story of the dog sleeping on the farmer's porch. The farmer is sitting in the rocking chair, and the dog is moaning in its sleep. The farmer's friend asks why the dog is moaning. "It's because the dog is lying on a protruding nail," the farmer replies. So the friend asks why the dog doesn't move. The farmer replies, "He will when it hurts enough." That describes a lot of people. They get in that comfort zone and don't move until it gets uncomfortable again.

Think of goal setting as two categories: move-toward goals and move-away goals. You need a clear understanding of both to maintain momentum and not rest too long on any one step.

1. Move-toward goals.

Move-toward goals are easy. These are the fun things in life, usually value-driven, and the most exciting to think about. They are things you want to move toward: primary homes, lake homes, children's educations, vacations, money in the bank, and so forth. The bigger the goal, the bigger the challenge, and the bigger the satisfaction that comes with accomplishing the goal. I feel bad for people who have never stretched themselves because they have never felt the satisfaction of rewards like these.

Move-toward goals are:

- Based on our most burning desires

- A vision for the future and long term in nature

- Almost always positive in nature

- About the Bountiful Life

- About our aspirations

- Sometimes so fantastic that we say them without really believing we can achieve them (which is where most of our achievement problems come into play)

These move-toward goals are the stuff dreams are made of.

It is hard for people to envision themselves different in the future. We are all a product of our past environment. Whether we had supportive or less supportive parents, came from a wealthy background or a modest one, or were instilled with confidence or left to feel insecure, the factors that shape us, I am told, are in place as early as age five. What chance do we have to change any of that?

But setting goals can help us change our destiny. Focusing on move-toward goals helps to paint a picture in our mind's eye of what life can be like for us and those we love. So we think about the summer cottage on the lake, the trips we will take with our families, the way we will live in retirement. The list goes on and on. Maintaining a lifelong image of these objectives is not easy and needs constant reinforcement. That is why we use pictures of things we desire to keep dreams alive. That is why we talk about our goals and dreams with loved ones.

2. Move-away goals.

In contrast, move-away goals are an external force that helps us move out of our comfort zones. The more we respond to move-away goals, the closer we will come to achieving the dreams of our move-toward goals. Move-away goals are both negative and positive. Negative move-away goals include unpaid bills, mounting credit card balances, late mortgage payments, and a tax bill from the IRS. These are all things that can be either debilitating or motivating. The motivation, however, is short term. Once we pay the bill, the motivation is over.

An example of a positive move-away goal is an agency contest. This provides an external motivation designed to move people to a higher level. An external move-away might be a bet with a friend to accomplish a specific goal over a period of time. Reps often make bets to reach a certain number of dials per day or a certain number of lives per month. These are often fun but are finite by design. They have limited impact and need periodic renewal. The negative move-aways will wear you down over time. The positive ones require that you give in to them and play the game. Negative move-aways drag you down — "pay the overdue bills or else" — and the positive ones lose their effect over time.

Move-away goals are those things you want to move away from, to avoid. To help you understand move-away goals, I will share a personal story previously known by only a couple of people in my life.

I was 17 years old, a senior in high school, and captain of the football team. Mt. Pleasant High School had been the state football champ for a record 10 consecutive years. I played on both sides of the ball, pulling right guard and middle linebacker. While I wasn't the biggest guy on the team by a long shot, I was strong and quick. I had great hopes to captain the team to its 11th state championship. In addition, I was really excited to find out from my coach that he had received several inquiries from colleges about my abilities, and I knew scouts were in the stands on Saturdays. We always played our preseason games against Massachusetts and Connecticut teams in hopes of playing the toughest games possible out of state.

When our regular season began, we were dominating with three wins and no losses, and I began to hear more about which colleges were watching me. There were some great schools, not the big football ones, but some good ones, even a couple of Ivy League schools. I thought, "Well let's first worry about getting in, and then I'll figure out how to stay in!" I came from humble beginnings, and I certainly didn't have the money to attend a private school, so a scholarship would have been an incredible gift.

In our fourth game, while playing defense, I was clipped in the backfield, and my knee twisted in a direction I knew wasn't good. On Saturday afternoon, October 4, 1964, my doctor told me that not only was my season over, but I also had not one but three torn ligaments. My football career and my hopes for a scholarship were over. I cried. I loved football, but what I had really been working for was a means to finance my education. I would have been only the second Hoopis to go to college. I was hospitalized for 10 days, wore a cast for three months, and attended games on crutches every Saturday as captain. I was a high school hero, but I lost my chance at attending a private school with a big name.

I attended the University of Rhode Island and made the best of it. It turned out to be a great school for me. I had a great experience, and today I am so happy that the turn of events led me to the industry and job I have loved so much.

Sometime between the hospital stay and graduation from college, I decided that when I married and had children, I wanted to

be able to let my children go to any school they wanted to and could get into, regardless of cost. I would do anything to make that happen! I wanted to avoid having my children experience the crushing realization that they could not afford to go to the school of their choice, so that became my move-away goal, plus it was value-based.

Once I got into this business, I could always look at my move-toward goals and get excited, but if I slowed down and stopped making the extra calls, I knew that atrophy might set in and I might not achieve the goals I had set for myself. I just had to move away from letting the unthinkable (not reaching that goal) happen. To this day, I believe that the thought of having to tell my kids they couldn't go to the school of their choice motivated me more than anything else, particularly when I might be finding it easier to accept the hardship of making a poor living than to accept the difficulties of making a better one.

I shared this concept of move-aways with a ClientBuilder group years ago. One member of the group told about his move-away, which was powdered milk. His parents used to buy powered milk and add water to it. It was much cheaper than fresh milk (and tasted it, too). He had a large family, and his parents did what they had to do to stretch a dollar. He said he worked hard so that he would never find himself having to buy powdered milk for his family, no matter what.

What is your "no matter what"? What will drive you when the move-toward goals get a little cloudy? What will force you to pick it up and get moving? What will ensure that you will use all your potential, not just a measured amount?

The interaction between move-toward goals and move-away goals is essential in helping us achieve our dreams. If you agree with my second rule of life, which is that we are all basically lazy, you will see how move-away goals can help us stay focused on move-toward goals. It is the combination of move-towards and move-aways that gives us lasting goal achievement.

To set meaningful goals, you first must create in your mind's eye a vision of the future. Where do I see myself at ages 30, 40, 50, and 60? How will I feel when I watch my child graduate from college? How will I feel

> "What you *get* by achieving your goals is not as important as what you *become* by achieving your goals."
>
> —Henry David Thoreau

in that summer home on the lake surrounded by my grandchildren? It is always about how you think you will feel because you are not there yet. Our ability to paint word pictures is important, and everyone should practice doing it.

So the next time you are WORK-ing in your car, try painting word pictures of your greatest goal. Can you describe the feeling of achievement? Can you describe that home in detail? Can you talk about retirement in word pictures? Henry David Thoreau said, "What you *get* by achieving your goals is not as important as what you *become* by achieving your goals." It's true.

We are motivated in two ways: internally and externally. Our move-toward goals involve internal motivation, and our move-away goals involve external motivation. A move-toward goal is driven by core inner values, while move-away goals are driven by external influences. Both are related in a meaningful way. No one I know of can, does, or should operate in either of these modes all the time. Remember that our business is merely the funding vehicle for everything else we want to do in our lives. We set business goals to help us achieve our most important dreams, the ones that complete us.

Every time we attain a move-away goal, whether it is paying a bill or winning a contest, we need to capture one of our burning desires and put a plan in place to achieve it. In other words, from the mountaintop of reaching a goal, we must look up to see our move-toward objectives. We can never see those from the valley of desperation, which is where we reside when we are surrounded by negative external influences. Comfort zones sap us of our courage. It's essential to goal achievement to learn to switch from external drivers to internal drivers at the right time.

After 40-plus years in this business and a lifetime of watching people, I have some ideas about what the keys to success are. One of the most important is not being afraid to dream, not being afraid to give in to the thought of working hard to achieve your goals, and not being afraid to let the external influences in your life lift you out of the valley of despair and mediocrity. Give in to your dreams and harness the challenges of both negative and positive external events to help you see the steps to a brighter future. Self-help author, businessman, and philanthropist W. Clement Stone said, "The reason so few people are successful is no one has yet found a way for someone to sit down and slide uphill."

The famous psychologist and concentration camp survivor Viktor Frankl said, "Life can be pulled by goals just as surely as it can be pushed by drives." Think of move-towards as goals and move-aways as drivers.

Paint a Mental Picture of Your Goals

Attending an MDRT meeting is always an uplifting experience. I love how all of these individuals come together with a common bond to improve their skills and their lives so they can help others.

As always, a common theme among top performers is the importance of goal setting, visualization, self-discipline, hard work, and record-keeping. The best reps know that measurement improves performance. Anything we can measure, we can improve.

In 1954, Roger Bannister broke the four-minute-mile barrier. Up until he broke that record with remarkable effort, doctors thought the human heart might explode if pushed to that kind of limit. Amazingly, as soon as the record was broken, more than a dozen other runners accomplished the same result within a year of Roger.

During MDRT meetings, I always hoped that our reps were listening to the speakers, many of whom have broken personal barriers on par with a four-minute mile, and were thinking, "If he can do it, so can I!"

In author David L. Cook's audio CD version of *Seven Days in Utopia: Golf's Sacred Journey*, he shares a great story about his work as a sports psychologist training and working with many athletes and coaches, including the San Antonio Spurs and many big-name college coaches.

Early in his career, Dr. Cook's team was doing some research on mental toughness. He wanted to examine what focus could do when people were tested to their maximum abilities. He set up a treadmill test in which his subject, an ex-Marine, was to run until complete exhaustion. He set up the test in a bare room with nothing on the walls and asked the Marine to give him 100 percent — the perfect words to say to a Marine. The Marine collapsed after 26 minutes. When the Marine recovered, he asked how he did. Dr. Cook responded: "Unbelievable! You went 27:50! That is as good as the top quartile of our tests. Do you think you can get to 28 minutes next time?"

The Marine, not knowing he had really run for only 26 minutes, responded, "Of course. I am a Marine."

Dr. Cook then gave him a big piece of paper with "28" written on it in red ink and asked him to look at it every day.

The next week, the Marine returned and was ready for the challenge. This time, Dr. Cook put a big clock right in front of the Marine's face with a big red line at 28 minutes. He then told the Marine to get to 28 minutes (not "give me 100 percent"). At around 26 minutes, the Marine showed signs of collapsing again but fought through it, and as the clock passed 28:07, the Marine collapsed. After his recovery, Dr. Cook praised him on how well he did. He then asked him to return again next week to see if he could get to 28:30. The Marine agreed and returned the next week to the treadmill. This time, there was no clock. The Marine asked Dr. Cook, "Where is the clock?" Dr. Cook responded that he did not need a clock this time. "Just give me 100 percent."

The Marine collapsed again just before 26 minutes. And again, after he recovered, he asked how he did. Dr. Cook responded "Unbelievable! You made it to 28:45! Do you think you can do it one more time next week?"

The Marine responded again, not as enthusiastic this time, "Of course. I am a Marine." Dr. Cook gave him a sheet again, and this time wrote "28:45" in red and asked him to look at it every day. The following week, the Marine returned for the final time, and again there was a clock right in front of him. As he got on the treadmill for the last time, Dr. Cook said to him, "Let's see 28:45!" As you might have guessed, the Marine made it just past 28:45.

The point of the story is this: We must have a focus and a vision for our goals. Sometimes just "giving it 100 percent" is not enough because it isn't really 100 percent. Our mind thinks it is, but it isn't. This is why we set daily, weekly, and monthly goals. We can all do much better. We can all do more than we believe we can. We just need to focus on the target, and then do whatever it takes to accomplish our most amazing future.

Picture Your Amazing Future

Since being introduced to the concept of my "amazing future," I have spent a lot of time thinking about it. It keeps getting bigger and more exciting all the time. After all, when you put your mind to something, there are seemingly no limits. Testing what needs to be done to get there gives me weekly goals I can get excited about.

Dr. Cooper also spoke at one of our client-appreciation events a few years ago and said something that resonated with me: "Most people would rather have a problem they can't solve than a solution they don't like." Do you ever find yourself blaming the economy, the war, the president, a broken relationship, or something from your past that is causing the problems or distractions in your life that prevent you from realizing your amazing future?

Or do you say, "If I see enough people or get enough fact-finders or dial the phone enough or get the right kind of referrals, everything will be OK?" That is our biggest challenge — taking action to get the solution that we know involves more effort but will solve our issues. Whatever your issues are, ask yourself what solution would solve them. You are talented, intelligent, hardworking, and committed. You can do it. If you weren't, you would not be where you are today. What most of us don't do is continually test which solution will get us to the next level or help us reach our goals. Each of you knows what the solution is for you to achieve your goals and dreams. Choose the solution.

Dr. Cooper also said, "What got you here won't get you there, to the next place. What got you here might not be enough to keep you here." It's up to you to keep on choosing solutions as each new challenge presents itself.

In our profession, we look at each new year somewhat differently than the average person. For us, it's about more than a fresh start. It's about setting *new* goals, meeting *new* challenges, and acquiring *new* clients. Many people in other professions don't share this anxiety. They go to work, do what they are told, and pick up a check. I'm not saying that isn't important; I'm saying they are not making it happen for themselves.

We have to measure ourselves against our potential — what we feel we are capable of doing. Do you really measure yourself against your potential, or do you measure yourself against what is just enough — enough to pay your bills, enough to make minimum standards? Those measurements are not about potential. They are about maintaining the status quo or being better than someone else, but they are not about your potential. What exactly are you saving your potential for? You know you cannot take it with you. I challenge you to think differently and to set some goals that are truly a stretch for you.

Start thinking about move-toward, value-driven goals. When achieved, they will help you attain your amazing future. So what does the amazing future look like to you? My amazing future, before I retired, meant continuing to lead a world-class organization, having a worldwide impact on the industry, while spending more time with family and friends.

Many years ago, I asked the reps in ClientBuilders to close their eyes and think about the image that came to them when I said a number of phrases, including Tiananmen Square, Olympic gold, Mount Everest, and space shuttle. In every case, reps reported having a very clear image of the events associated with each phrase. Then I asked them what image they saw when I said, "Your success." Most people have neglected to create this image in their mind. If you haven't done this, then how will you know when you achieve it? The first thing you need to do is create this image. Is it you standing on the dock of your summer cottage? Is it you sitting in the library of your magnificent home? Is it you on stage at your company annual meeting making a presentation? If someone were to ask you what your success looks like, what would you say? What do you see? Try it now!

> Successful people have a clear and definite connection between what they think about, where they are going, and what they do every day to achieve it.

Next, you need to work backward from that image — in every detail. What will it take to achieve your goal? How much money will you need for that cottage on the lake? What production level will be necessary? How many lives, how many new clients, how many referrals, how many phone calls? To achieve your goals in five or 10 years, you have to break it down to the very next activity you perform. Once the image is there, everything you do needs to be connected to that outcome — not some of the time, all of the time. This is the fundamental difference between those who reach their potential and those who don't. The successful people have a clear and definite connection between what they think about, where they are going, and what they do every day to achieve it.

So change your thinking. Make what you want to achieve real. Remember that is not measured by the amount of money, but instead by what the money can buy. Making the connection between money and how it helps you reach your goals is a key component of your success.

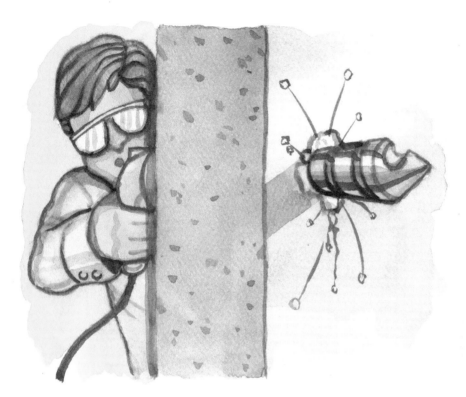

What makes this so difficult for people to grasp and why so few perform beyond their *needs*, as opposed to their *potential*, is because the game isn't fair. The effort needed varies among people, and the definition of potential does, too. Yet everyone can achieve their potential. As I discussed in an earlier chapter, you have to drill through the wall to get everything you want out of life. Your job is to choose the type of drill bits you use. You must commit to lifelong learning and hone your ability to win the trust of new clients. The stronger they are, the faster they work. But remember the toughest part of all: You don't know how thick your wall is. It's different for each person. If every wall were the same, our profession would be more about endurance than achievement. More like those who work in other industries who endure the day, the week, the month, get the paycheck, and go home. You have the challenge of great achievement to drive you or derail you. You get to choose. Don't put down the drill and give up with only another day's work to do.

Make What You Are Worth, Not What You Need

In 2010, I was at an industry meeting in which we were discussing productivity. One of the people at the table made an observation. He said, "Reps have a way of deciding how much they will make in a given year and then go about doing it. No more, no less. They just know what they want to make." This is true for many of you.

I have always said, "You either make what you need to make or what you think you are worth." That is only slightly different than what my friend said. Some reps make what they think they are worth, while others work for just the amount they need to pay their bills. For the ones who decide how much they will make, they make it by 10 percent more or 10 percent less. But for those of you who know the value you bring to your clients, who know how much you know, who care enough to be the best you can be, the sky is the limit.

Get past the urge to be just you and instead be someone special.

What is your number? What is your goal? Are you calculating what you need to make or what you are worth? If you are falling short, what about your commitment to help more people is not taking place? Find the courage to do things differently. Courageous activity — stepping it up — makes a difference. Risk embarrassing yourself. Laugh at yourself. Be willing to try something new and make mistakes.

Hal Prince, the famous Broadway producer, said, "Anyone who hasn't had a failure is an amateur." Get past the urge to be just you and instead be someone special. Commit to taking that next step in your career and make a difference in the lives of your clients and family. Don't waste this opportunity.

Remember that goal setting requires character — that is, the ability to carry out a resolution long after the emotion that caused you to make it has left you.

If you can connect the dots, you can be extremely successful. These are the dots:

- Make what you are worth, not what you need to make.

- Recognize important reasons to do more for yourself and your family.

- Have the character to stick with it for an extended period of time.

Connect these dots, and you will be on your way to the Bountiful Life.

My Father Owned
a Grocery Store

**"No great thing is
created suddenly."**

—Epictetus

I became connected to the pursuit of the Bountiful Life because it is the perfect payoff for a hard job done well. The Bountiful Life isn't even an option for some people because it requires both the time and money to enjoy the things you want to do with the people you love. Some people get the time but no money, and some get the money but no time. Our business, for those who do it in an efficient, effective, and persistent manner, offers both to all who excel at it.

My hope is that by sharing some of my lessons and insights more of you will get there. There were many lessons in my early life that were so important. Working in our family grocery store, the Four Corners Market, with my parents was an incredible experience. I witnessed sacrifice, suffering, success, and satisfaction all under one roof. Based on all these lessons, I even thought about titling this book, "My Father Owned a Grocery Store."

Learning my life lessons early certainly shaped who I was. We lived the three Rs: respect, responsibility, and resourcefulness. I learned that turning the doorknob on your own business was worth some enormous sacrifices. I learned that the customer was always right, unless he lied. I learned that the store must always be open when you say it will be open, no excuses. I learned you gave 100 percent, whether hurt or sick — or both. Sick days weren't for entrepreneurs; they were for employees.

Then I grew up. I learned that these life lessons gave me an advantage in life. Those lessons applied to school and, more importantly, in college. I learned to balance school, work, and play while attending college. Later, as a young intern, I learned that those traits stood out in the world. I felt different, older, and more mature than my colleagues. I knew I had an advantage (which was a good thing with grades like mine).

These lessons helped me as a young rep as I interacted with clients who were older than me and gave advice to those my age. Then, as a leader, I realized that I did know some secrets to success, and I had the conviction to share those insights.

Giving up was never an option. Anything worth having was worth working for. I discovered there were two struggles in life, one for success and one of mediocrity. I was able to choose the struggle for success because I knew that struggle had a better outcome. I learned that potential was a God-given gift and unused potential was a sin. And while it's always hard to know if you are living up to your potential, everyone seems to know when they are not. You just need to form the habit of asking yourself at the end of each day, "On a scale of 1 to 10, how did I do in reaching my potential today?"

My advice is to go back and read the book again and again. There are so many nuggets in here — a mindset to uncover. Understanding how important the Bountiful Life is will trigger *extra* ordinary activities and behaviors. Don't miss this opportunity. This book was written by someone who has lived it. This book was written by someone who knows that building a career is not easy, but incredibly worth it. Because as I have said, it is the funding vehicle for everything we want to do in life.

Never be afraid to dream. Never be afraid to make a mistake. Never stop the pursuit of knowledge. Do this and watch what can happen for you.

When I was just 14 years old, I saw a cartoon I have had with me for over 50 years. It was a picture of a hobo resting under a tree watching a distinguished man puff a cigar as he passed by in a limousine. The caption reads, "There except for me, goes I." I guess that move-away made sense to me, because I never wanted to say anything close to that.

When I die, I want my tombstone to read, "Here lies Harry, his potential all used up!" As opposed to, "Here lies Harry, his potential still intact!"

Which will it be for you? Are you willing to do whatever it takes, as long as it's legal and moral, to achieve the Bountiful Life? I know your answer is yes. Now go out there and get it!

Resources for Lifelong Learning

Resources

The following resources are recommended as development tools for sales professionals and their support teams.

Hoopis Performance Network
www.hoopis.com

Hoopis Performance Network (HPN) is an online resource for sales professionals and organizational leaders in insurance and financial services. The site provides training programs, seminars, and consulting and coaching services, as well as products that include assessment tools, books, audio CDs, videos, and field resources. Based on more than 30 years of industry leadership experience, these proven resources have been created and enhanced in HPN's very own "living laboratory."

Highlights include:

- *Trustworthy Selling*, an award-winning training program developed by HPN and LIMRA International; this relationship-oriented sales training program engages prospects and clients on their own terms and includes field-tested communication techniques and sales strategies

- Assessment tools including "Understanding and Adapting Your Sales Style" and "Top Producer Mindset Differential"

- The Virtual Coach, a resource that helps you prepare for an appointment by spending five to 10 minutes online watching a top producer or consultant address the very topic you need

The LIFE Foundation
www.lifehappens.org

The mission of the Life and Health Insurance Foundation for Education (LIFE) is to educate the public about the need for insurance and to motivate them to make good choices for themselves, their businesses, and their loved ones. Their programs, campaigns, and resources can help your prospective clients understand their insurance needs and motivate them to take action to achieve a secure financial future.

Highlights include:

- RealLIFEstories that demonstrate the importance of insurance products, proper planning, and how an insurance professional made an extraordinary difference in their clients' lives; the stories are featured in online commercials, videos, and flyers

- Calculators that clients and prospects can access online to determine their coverage needs

- Downloadable guides to educate prospective clients on products, including their purpose, features, benefits, and more

MDRT
www.mdrt.org

Founded in 1927, MDRT provides its members with resources to improve their technical knowledge, sales, and client service while maintaining a culture of high ethical standards. Through its many professional development programs, services, and products, MDRT provides opportunities for qualifying members to gain new and unique insights into all aspects of expanding their business.

Highlights include:

- The MDRT annual meeting, open to all qualifying members

- The MDRT Power Center, containing information on sales ideas, objection guides, closing, prospecting, estate planning, practice management, marketing, and branding

- Topical Web seminars and an extensive library offered at no cost to members to help enhance personal and professional growth

National Association of Insurance and Financial Advisors
www.naifa.org

Founded in 1890 as the National Association of Life Underwriters (NALU), NAIFA is one of the nation's oldest and largest associations representing the interests of insurance professionals. NAIFA advocates for a positive legislative and regulatory environment, enhances its members' business and professional skills, and promotes ethical conduct.

Highlights include:

- Serving as the exclusive research sponsor of *Advisor 2020: The Forces and Opportunities Shaping the Financial Services Advisor of the Future,* and providing resources and programs to help agents and advisors adapt their practices to the rapidly changing financial services landscape

- The Leadership in Life Institute (LILI) six-month program that fosters deep personal growth, strong practice development, and broader and more effective leadership skills

- The Young Advisors Team (YAT), which helps newer advisors grow and thrive as sales professionals in insurance and financial services while deepening their involvement in the industry

The American College
www.theamericancollege.edu

Founded in 1927, The American College is the nation's oldest and largest nontraditional institution for higher learning devoted exclusively to the academic study of financial services. An accredited institution, The American College offers 10 professional designations and two master's programs.

Highlights include:

- Chartered Life Underwriter (CLU) designation
- Chartered Financial Consultant (ChFC) designation
- Certified Financial Planner (CFP) designation